Contents

Western Area

Introduction

Really Good Walks are interesting walks that always go to the highest point. They get there, and back, in as straightforward a way as possible, avoiding pointy edges, steep drops, scree runs and the worst of the crowds.

The mountains of the English Lake District provide a superb variety of walks for fellwalkers of all ages and abilities from lengthy circuits of high peaks to shorter outings over lower heights. Whilst there can sometimes be a perception that visiting the higher peaks involves more challenging outings traversing exposed ridges and rough fellsides, this is not necessarily so. By careful choice of route, walkers who prefer to do so, may visit most of the best places in Lakeland, including the majority of its summits, using straightforward paths without encountering any particular difficulty.

So, in this guide you will find a collection of *Really Good Walks* which provide straightforward ways to visit one or more Wainwright summits. The mountains climbed are both high ones, including the highest of them all, Scafell Pike, and low ones, which although less grand, offer some of the very best views of valleys and lakes encompassed by fine mountains. All are circular walks, generally between four and eight miles long and therefore suitable for a half or full-day walk; the timings given presume an easy pace with many stops for breathers, photographs and, on full-day walks, sandwiches. They are spread across all corners of the region and together give a good picture of the wide diversity of the National Park's natural beauty. Where there is scope for doing so without compromising the quality of the walk, quieter routes are always chosen, but sadly, for the more popular tops, especially those that have featured on television, there are sometimes no such things.

Whilst the routes described have been chosen to prefer smoothness to roughness underfoot, from time to time you will encounter sections of path which, because of the passage of many boots and the ravages of the weather, have become ribbons of unpleasant loose stone and are the least attractive of the possible onward ways. In these situations, there is sometimes a choice to be made between staying on the path and dealing with rough walking, or escaping from it onto easier ground. Thus within the walk descriptions you will find places where it is suggested that an off-path route is used to circumvent unpleasantness or difficulties. It is important to stress that off-path means properly, ideally several yards, off the path, well away from already worn areas. It does not mean just moving onto the margins of the erosion where the walking will often be easier but where you, and everybody else doing the same thing, will be contributing in a very real way to even more erosion and the broadening of the path scar.

Happily, in addition to finding some seriously worn paths, you will increasingly encounter places where previously eroded footpaths have been repaired, the damage to the landscape halted and the progress of walkers made easier. This excellent restoration work is being undertaken, with the help of many volunteers, by the National Park Authority, the National Trust and other organisations; details are on the web (**www.fixthefells.com**) if you'd like to learn more and help this splendid work to continue.

Safety, of course, is the first thing to think about before setting out into the hills, and there is no better guidance than that in the *How to stay safe and enjoy the fells* leaflet produced by the Lake District Search and Mountain Rescue Association and available, with lots of other useful information, on their website at **www.ldsamra.org.uk**. However, perhaps the greatest single factor contributing to hazard-free walking is the one which is most difficult to arrange – calm, clear, dry weather. To give yourself the best chance of getting it right, the Lake District Weatherline issues a daily forecast which is available on the web (**www.lakedistrictweatherline.co.uk**) or by phone (0844 846 2444). Also, BBC Radio Cumbria broadcasts a generally helpful forecast for the county with specific mention of expected conditions on the fells at, among other times, 0632, 0732 and 0832 on weekdays.

However, even having taken careful note of all the forecasts in the world, there will still be times on the hills when the weather unexpectedly deteriorates in a serious way. Heavy rain is no fun, but hill fog that rolls in and limits visibility to not much further than your own boots can lead to serious navigational problems, even on trodden routes. You should therefore never set out onto the hills without the appropriate OS 1:25,000 map plus a compass and the ability to use the two of them with total confidence to navigate back to the valley in which is located your bed for the night, or your transport thereto.

Trekking poles are unreservedly recommended, not only for the extra support and balance they provide, but also, because they enable your arms to contribute to the overall upward push when ascending, they take some load off your leg muscles and generally ease the climb.

Public transport in the National Park has improved significantly in recent years and use of the bus rather than the car must be a good idea where this is practicable. However, relying on catching a bus which only runs three or four times a day for the return to base at the end of a day's walk can be nerve-racking, and most of us will use cars to access walk start points. The routes described thus all start from proper parking places, with nearby alternatives, where available, also described. Where there is a choice, quieter parking areas have been chosen but these are generally hard to find, and the best advice that can be given is to arrive early, especially on busier days.

The walks in this guide have been grouped into four sections depending on the locations of their starting points:

Northern for walks starting in the Borrowdale and Newlands valleys, and in, around and to the north of Keswick;

Southern for walks starting around Ambleside, Langdale, Grasmere, Coniston and in the south-east;

Eastern for walks starting around Ullswater and Haweswater;

Western for walks starting in the western valleys – Buttermere, Loweswater, Ennerdale, Eskdale and Wasdale.

Each walk is accompanied by an outline diagram. These are included for general orientation and to give an overview of the walk; they are not substitutes for a proper map. In the diagrams, the walking route is shown as a bold intermittent line, and access roads to the starting point are shown as lighter continuous lines, with road numbers shown where appropriate.

May you enjoy many wonderful days on the hills.

Meanwhile, in this April month, Francis and his son David rode together [from Rosthwaite] to Ravenglass to stay, for several nights, with brother Harcourt. They rode over the Stye Head Pass and down into Wasdale. David rode on Caesar and Francis on a little shaggy horse that he called Walpole because he had a belly and was cynically indifferent to any morality. The little horses picked their way very carefully up the hill with deliberate slowness.

No one hurried them. The day was grey and still with little pools of sunlight in a dark sky. The hills had snow on their tops, but in the valleys the larches were beginning to break into intense green flame. As they wound up the Pass, the hills gathered about them, not grandly and with arrogant indifference as larger hills do in other countries, but with intimacy and friendliness as though they liked human beings and were interested in their fates.

Hugh Walpole writing in *Rogue Herries*
of a journey made on the 10th of April 1737

Walk 1
A bird's-eye view of Keswick

This is a short walk from near the centre of Keswick to the summit of Latrigg, from where there are fine views over the town to the Borrowdale, Newlands and Bassenthwaite fells. The return route wanders through Brundholme Woods in the company of the River Greta, and provides a surprise view of an impressive piece of civil engineering. Apart from one short section of the ascent, the gradients are easy throughout.

A short part of this walk makes use of a recently constructed "Limited Mobility Path" which provides access from the car park at the top of Gale Road (NY 280253), for "strong and confident wheelchair users", to the excellent viewpoint near the summit of Latrigg; further information on this and other accessible routes in the National Park, is at **www.lakedistrict.gov.uk/mileswithoutstiles**.

Summit visited	Latrigg (1207ft/368m)
Start	Keswick Leisure Pool (Old Railway Station)
Distance	5.75 miles/9.25km
Height gain	1050ft/320m
Time	3 hours
Map	OS Explorer OL4 (North-western)
Facilities	There are toilets on the old platform

Parking: Park behind the old railway station, adjacent to the "Leisure Pool and Fitness Centre" in Keswick (NY 270238). To reach the parking area, follow the brown signs to the Leisure Pool either along Brundholme Road from the A5271 at Great Crosthwaite, or along

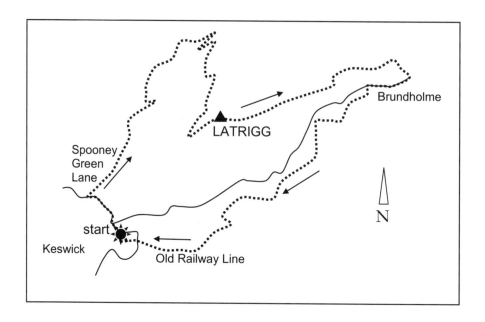

Station Road. Turn into the Leisure Pool car park from the mini-roundabout and keep left to drive along the old railway line (signed Keswick Railway Footpath) with what was Keswick Railway Station, and is now part of the Station Hotel, on your right. The first three bays on the left say you can only park there if you are using the Pool, but beyond these are a number of other bays in which you can park free of charge.

Alternatively, on Brundholme Road, approaching from the A5271, there are wider sections on the left after the old railway bridge piers and opposite the houses around the bottom of Spooney Green Lane; starting from here, the first few sentences of the walk will move to its end. The walk may also be done, without adding significantly to its length, from any of the Keswick car parks by walking down Station Road and leaving it on the left (signed Railway Footpath) where the road bends right and continuing to the right of the Leisure Pool building to reach its car park.

The walk

Leave the car park by the vehicle access road, cross the mini-roundabout and go up the short flight of wooden steps opposite. Turn left onto the path running parallel to the road, go through a gate and continue across a narrow metalled lane. Our destination, Latrigg, is on the right, with the Skiddaw massif to its left. Where the path ends, cross the road and continue on the pavement along Briar Rigg in front of some houses. In a couple of hundred yards, turn right up Spooney Green Lane (signed Skiddaw), continuing over the A66, through a waymarked kissing gate, and past an information board, where the way gets steeper. Ignore paths off left and right and continue straight on. Skiddaw dominates the skyline ahead.

A little way further on, after the track has become less wide and less steep, at a fork keep left to visit the viewpoint of Ewe How, from where there is a panorama of the North-Western Fells, from Dale Head above Derwentwater round to Lord's Seat above Bassenthwaite Lake. Immediately beyond the viewpoint keep left again on the lower path, to reach firstly a kissing gate and then another information board at Gale Ghyll Woods. Beyond this, keep left and walk by the fence along the top side of a plantation, ignoring the path descending into the trees. Then, 50yds past the end of the plantation, turn sharp right on

Looking to Derwentwater and Borrowdale from Latrigg

a clear path (signed Latrigg summit) which zig-zags up via two further hairpin bends to a junction. Here we join the new Limited Mobility path from Gale Road car park, on which we continue to reach a seat from which there is the best panorama on the fell – of Derwentwater, Bassenthwaite Lake and the hills beyond, as well as a bird's eye view of Keswick.

Here the surfaced path ends as we turn left to continue to the top of Latrigg. The path passes near to or over three rocky bumps, of which the middle one is probably the actual summit, although not a single stone marks the highest point. Continue past some lone trees and through a gate onto a less-clear grass path which descends the field ahead. Just before reaching a cross-fence, the path drops down half-left to a track by a gate. Go through and continue down to a gate with a stile and a finger-post. Go through and turn right down the narrow stony tarmac lane, past a "Road Ahead Closed" sign, to begin the return to Keswick.

Soon a wood is seen on the left. A fence runs down the hillside beside it. Immediately beyond this fence, turn left down a narrow path beside it to join a broader path at a zig-zag. Follow this broader path round to the right, dropping gently into the wood; ignore the smaller path which goes straight down the slope by a fence. At a fork, ignore a sign with a green tree pointing left downhill, and keep right to continue high above the river on an undulating and sometimes muddy path. Ignore all paths running off right or left and keep ahead on the main path. This drops briefly to the riverside and then passes under the impressive high bridge which carries the A66 high above over the river, before arriving at the Brundholme Woods information panel at Brigham Forge. Go through the kissing gate and turn left across the old stone bridge over the River Greta. Turn right up the concrete road, and in 100yds go left up some steps by a "Children Ahead" sign, following a finger-post "Keswick Railway Footpath". Turn right onto the old railway trackbed and follow this for ten minutes to arrive back exactly at the car park by the Leisure Pool.

Walk 2
The Outerside – Barrow Ridge

The traverse of this pleasant low ridge which rises above the village of Braithwaite provides a straightforward excursion with good views. The majority of the uphill walking is on an easily graded old mine track, and the majority of the descent on a delightful grassy highway overlooking the Vale of Keswick and the Skiddaw massif.

Summits visited	**Outerside (1863ft/568m)** **Stile End (1467ft/447m)** **Barrow (1493ft/455m)**
Start	**Uzzicar**
Distance	**5 miles/8km**
Height gain	**1900ft/580m**
Time	**3.25 hours**
Map	**OS Explorer OL4 (North-western)**
Facilities	**In Braithwaite village there are pubs/hotels and a shop. There are also a café and a shop on the campsite**

Parking: Park on the roadside near Uzzicar (NY 232218). From Braithwaite, follow the signs to Newlands, taking the right fork beyond the village (signed Newlands, Buttermere). Shortly past a cattle grid there is (i) parking on a long roadside lay-by on the right, (ii) space for two cars on the left immediately beyond the access track to Uzzicar Farm House, and (iii) a large parking space on the left at Stoneycroft.

The walk
From the long lay-by, continue away from Braithwaite past Uzzicar, and take the stony track which leaves the road on the right opposite the parking at Stoneycroft (low Public Footpath sign). Keep right at two forks

to continue above and to the right of Stonycroft Gill. Barrow, over which we will descend, is to our right, and Outerside, our initial objective is ahead. The hill on the left, across the stream, is Causey Pike.

After about a mile on the track, the gradient eases, there is an old ruined sheepfold on the left and the valley opens out; Outerside is now slightly behind us on our right. A little further on, just over a small rise, turn sharp right at a pile of stones and follow the thin clear path which crosses the damp, shallow depression, and then winds pleasantly the short distance up to the summit of Outerside. From here there is an excellent view of the higher mountains around the head of Coledale, the huge south-east face of Grisedale Pike across the valley being particularly impressive.

Continue north-eastwards to begin the descent of the ridge, during which our next destination, Stile End is clearly seen ahead, with Barrow beyond it and to its right. The way ahead is clear; where the path forks two-thirds of the way down, the right-hand way is probably easier.

At the far end of the depression, where the ground begins to rise, again there is a choice of paths. Either way will do, but preferably go left to contour round on a clear path which swings right. Then go round a boggy bit to pick up the path rising beyond it and heading up towards the

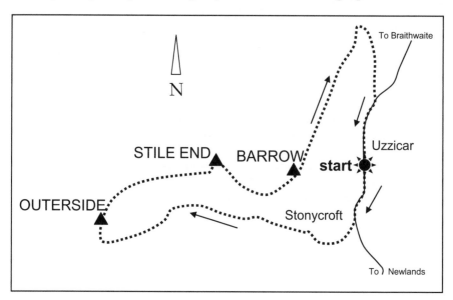

Sail and Crag Hill from the slopes of Outerside

highest point on the skyline. From here a clear path goes forward, swinging left to reach the top of Stile End.

Leave the top east of south on a path which is initially vague but quickly becomes very clear as it drops down the short distance to Barrow Door. Continue ahead taking the obvious path up Barrow – clearly seen during the descent. Cross the compact top of Barrow, which Wainwright describes as "overlooking a scene as fair as any in the kingdom", and continue on the clear, well-worn path down the ridge towards Braithwaite. On the descent there is a magnificent view ahead of Skiddaw, with Bassenthwaite to the left and Blencathra to the right, unfortunately a bit spoilt by the sight and noise of traffic on the A66 below. At the bottom of the main slope is a T-junction with a low signpost (right to Newlands; left to Braithwaite).

Take the right-hand way which runs a virtually level course in bracken above trees and then gently descends to join the Braithwaite to Newlands road a couple of hundred yards on the Newlands side of the cattle grid. Continue ahead to the car.

Walk 3
Grisedale Pike

Grisedale Pike is an eye-catching feature in the Keswick skyline and in the panorama as the town is approached from the east. This walk provides a way of visiting its summit which avoids the crowds and the worst of the erosion, and indeed 520ft/160m of ascent by starting from near the top of Whinlatter Pass. Following a short section in the forest, the ascent makes use of the delightful grassy ridge of Hobcarton End; the return is via by the easy slopes of the neighbouring north-east ridge. An extension of this short walk around the top of Hobcarton Crag to Hopegill Head is highly recommended.

Summits visited	Grisedale Pike (2593ft/791m) Hopegill Head (2525ft/770m)
Start	Revelin Moss car park, near the top of Whinlatter Pass
Distance	5.5 miles/8.75km
Height gain	2340ft/710m
Time	5 hours
Map	OS Explorer OL4 (North-western)
Facilities	At the Visitor Centre are toilets, a shop, café, and, from Easter to the end of August, a video-link to the osprey nesting site. Probably of less interest to users of this book are two more recent additions; "Go Ape", a perambulation through the tree canopy on various forms of walkways and cable-runs, and an extensive network of mountain biking trails with bike hire facilities

Skipping the trip to Hopegill Head and back will reduce these figures by 2 miles/3.25km, 750ft/230m and around 1.5 hours.

Parking: Travelling over Whinlatter Pass (B5292) from Braithwaite, there are a number of Forest Commission car parks. Park on the Revelin Moss car park (NY 209243) which is 2 miles/3.25km from Braithwaite, and is reached shortly before the entrance to the main Visitor Centre car park.

The walk

Leave the car park by walking back down the access road a very short distance to Junction 43. Here turn left to go round the vehicle barrier and along the forest track, which is also National Cycle Route 71. A forest cycleway joins from the left, and, further on, leaves again to the right; both junctions have many strange signs for cyclists. At a junction of tracks (Junction 41) go sharp right uphill (still on Cycle Route 71), and in 80yds take the clear path on the left which climbs through the trees.

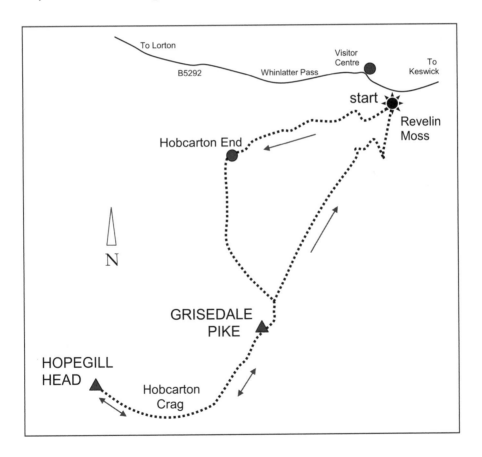

Immediately there is a fork; go left and climb quite steeply, keeping left if in doubt.

The path soon emerges from the thick forest into a lightly planted area and then, leaving the trees behind, swings left to climb clearly and charmingly through the heather on the slightly narrowing ridge. As the gradient eases, the path forks; go right to the cairn for the extensive view. From left to right this takes in Hopegill Head, our second objective, and its ridge over Ladyside Pike, the Loweswater Fells, with the Isle of Man above, the West Cumbrian Plain, Criffel across the Solway, Graystones, Broom Fell, Lord's Seat, Skiddaw, Blencathra, the Pennines, the Helvellyn ridge, and our immediate destination, Grisedale Pike. Wind turbines are much in evidence.

Continuing along the ridge, the path becomes almost level for a while, crossing a fence at a stile. It then drops into a slight depression before tackling the slope beyond. Climbing past a cairn, the rising path is initially unclear but then can be clearly seen zig-zagging its way up the easy slope. As the ground begins to level, the path again disappears but over on the left will be seen a broken wall with periodic old fence posts. Drift left to this wall and cross it to find a path on its far side (which is our return route). Turn right uphill. Shortly the main route from Braithwaite joins from the left and the path goes right to quickly arrive at the summit of Grisedale Pike. The view is superb.

Having taken in the view you could skip the rest of this paragraph and head off back down, but having got here with so little effort it would be a shame to miss the trip to Hopegill Head and back – all clearly in view from Grisedale Pike. So, continue over the summit on the only clear path, which descends by the broken wall to an initial depression and then traverses a subsidiary summit. Beyond this, keep right at the fork and continue round the rim of Hobcarton Crag to cross a second depression before rising to the shapely peak of Hopegill Head. There are tracks over to the left for those wishing to keep away from the edge. Return to Grisedale Pike the same way.

Leave the summit of Grisedale Pike the same way as you arrived, almost immediately picking up signs of the broken wall on the left which shortly, at old iron fence posts, turns left. Here at the wall corner the main path goes straight ahead to Braithwaite and our route turns left with the

The path from Grisedale Pike to Hopegill Head

broken wall. The mostly grassy path then follows the wall directly down to a gate into the forest.

Go through onto the forest track (where there is a Grisedale Pike sign pointing back the way you have come) and turn right. At a junction of tracks (Junction 42), go right. Where the track swings right at a cycling direction post, go left on a footpath past a yellow waymarker and follow this to a footbridge. Cross it, go left, rise to join the forest track and continue for two minutes back to the car park.

Walk 4
Secret tarns and fine views

Seathwaite Fell is unique in the District as its commonly accepted summit is not at its highest point, nor arguably at its best viewpoint. This varied and interesting ramble explores the extensive summit of the fell which, although itself of modest height, is encircled by higher and grander hills. Here, mostly in solitude and silence, you can wander at leisure, visiting the fell's many tops, discovering its hidden tarns, and taking in splendid views of Lakeland's grandest mountains and valleys.

The rambling summit plateau of the fell, which gives the walk great charm and interest on a clear day, makes this an outing which is unsuitable for misty conditions.

Summits visited	Seathwaite Fell (1970ft/601m) Great Slack (2073ft/632m)
Start	Seathwaite
Distance	5.5 miles/8.75km
Height gain	1760ft/540m
Time	5.5 hours
Map	OS Explorer OL4 (North-western)
Facilities	There are toilets on the left as you enter the farmyard at the start of the walk. On recent visits, a tea shop in the farm buildings has been closed; the nearest refreshments then are in Seatoller

Parking: Park on one of the wide verges of the minor road approaching Seathwaite Farm at the southern end of the Borrowdale Valley (NY 235122). These spaces fill up quickly; those arriving later will have to park further back down the road and thus have a slightly longer walk.

The walk

Walk up to the end of the tarmac road and continue ahead between the farm buildings and on up the broad, stony track, signposted Esk Hause and Sty Head. Continue up the valley, with the River Derwent on your right, to Stockley Bridge. Cross the stone arched bridge, go through the gate and continue straight on. (The path going left by the wall is our return route.) The path climbs fairly steeply and soon becomes paved and stepped as it rises to a gate in the intake wall. Through the gate, continue on the clear path which follows a fence on its right above Styhead Gill. As the gradient eases, the path swings left away from the fence and the stream. Seathwaite Fell is now directly ahead, its summit guarded by a line of crags. Looking along these to the right, at the first break there is a shallow grassy gully running directly up the fellside; this is our line of ascent.

The path quickly reverts to running parallel to Styhead Gill and soon swings right onto a line which will bring it alongside the gill at the top of some small falls. However, some 150yds before actually reaching these falls, the path crosses a small side stream (marked but unnamed on the OS 1:25000 map) which runs down the fellside in a clear, shallow gulley which reaches the skyline at the first break in the crags coming in from the left. There is no other stream with which this may be confused. On its right hand side, a faint grass trod can be seen heading off up the slope besides it and, with a little imagination, continuing all the way to the skyline. Follow this trod. The way is a steepish but otherwise straight-forward climb on grass weaving between stones, and keeping fairly close to the stream.

As the climb continues, the trod becomes more intermittent, disappearing in wet patches, and zig-zagging to the right a time or two. If in doubt, continue to climb just to the right of the stream or, further up the slope, its dry gulley. Eventually the gradient eases as a grassy shelf is reached. The summit, although unseen, is now close, and the gulley on the left points directly to it. So, continue uphill, avoiding the worst of the stones, and generally maintaining direction in company with the gulley. Very soon the summit of Seathwaite Fell appears half-left, crowned with a prominent cairn, and with a clear thin trod heading across to it.

From the cairn there is an excellent view of high mountains, the nearest neighbours, moving leftwards from the Seathwaite valley, being Green and

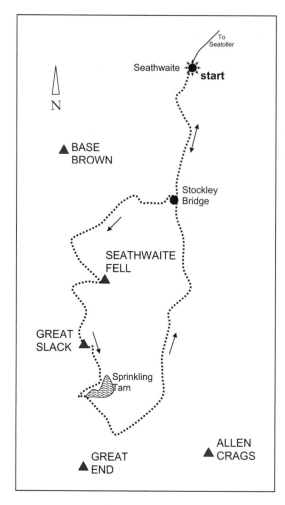

Great Gable, Lingmell, Great End and Glaramara. Beyond the Seathwaite valley is Borrowdale with the distinctive shapes of the diminutive Castle Crag in front of Derwentwater and the massive Skiddaw behind it.

Having soaked up the view and its accompanying silence, but before leaving the summit, it is helpful to get a picture of the geography of the upland plateau to the south-west, which has a lot of paths and quite a lot of cairns on high points. It is generally agreed that the summit on which we currently stand (1970ft/601m) is the summit of Seathwaite Fell, although it is not the highest point hereabouts. That distinction goes to Great Slack, a summit a hundred feet higher (2073ft/632m) on the low ridge to the south-west.

Our onward route takes us firstly to the cairned high point across the depression with the tarn, from where we walk left along the ridge, traversing Great Slack and then visiting a further high point (2070ft/631m) on the far left hand end of the ridge, before descending to Sprinkling Tarn.

So, find a way down off the summit rocks in the general direction of south-west to pick up the clear green path which crosses the depression to the right of the tarn. Then, where the path rises out of the depression

24

Great and Green Gable from Seathwaite Fell

and begins to swing left, leave it to continue ahead up the pathless grass slope to the cairn. On a warm day this is an excellent place to linger and enjoy the impressive view of Sty Head, Great Gable and of Lingmell – looking almost directly into the gash of Piers Gill.

Leave the cairn southwards along the low ridge. This is initially pathless but there is no difficulty in finding an easy grassy way. Then, across a minor depression the first "secret" tarn is found; a beautiful small piece of water with a heathery island. Pass the tarn and drop into a second depression, across which is a small rock face with a pile of stones on top. Pass to the left of the rock face, where you will find a faint path, and once round a wet bit and past a low crag on the right, strike right and follow a clear path leading up to the highest point – the top of Great Slack.

Continue southwards along the ridge to drop down to a Y-shaped tarn. Pass to the left of this and of a low crag, and then climb back up onto the ridge top and pick a way along between the rocks. Approaching where the ridge falls away quite steeply, you find another hidden tarn below and half-left. Look on the left for an easy way down to a thin path and turn right onto it. Follow the path round the right-hand side of the tarn and across its outlet, and then once again climb the grass to regain the ridge top. Walk along on grass to arrive at a pile of stones marking the final high point. This is the 631m point marked on the OS map. From here there is a good view of Wasdale Head and its unusual pattern of walls, with Lingmell rising on its left and Great Gable on its right.

Continue along the ridge, drop into a final depression and keep left to find a good way down pathless grass towards the tarn, turning right at the bottom of the slope onto a trod. When opposite the large promontory which sticks out into Sprinkling Tarn, trend left and head to a little pile of stones across a wetter section; trend left again to go round the left hand side of a wet hollow and of a little crag just beyond. Continue on, following a level course above the water on a good path, to join the major Sty Head to Esk Hause path exactly at the outflow from the tarn.

Turn left over the stepping stones and climb the rocky path. Soon, over the first rise, a path will be seen, beyond the gash of Ruddy Gill, going off left round the hillside – this is our return path. The way across the stream is not obvious from a distance but before long some stone steps descending to cross the beck to the very clear path beyond will be found. It is now simply a matter of following this path back down to the valley. Apart from one or two steps which require care, the way is easy, being mostly repaired. The path crosses a footbridge over Ruddy Gill and goes through a gate in the intake wall before arriving back at Stockley Bridge. Cross the bridge and retrace your steps by the river and through the farmyard to the car.

Walk 5
Ashness Bridge, High Seat
and Walla Crags

The walk described is a longish circuit which visits Ashness Bridge and then climbs to an excellent viewpoint at almost 2000ft/610m; the return is via an interesting ridge walk which leads to the popular Walla Crags. However, for days when poor weather or a shortage of time (or energy) rules out a high-level expedition, a shorter option which visits Ashness Bridge and Walla Crags, but short-cuts the higher ground, is also worthwhile. The first 1 mile/1.75km of the two alternatives is the same, offering the possibility of making a final decision on which to tackle depending on the turn of the weather. The longer route should be left alone in mist, after heavy rain, or at any time if your boots let in water.

Summits visited	**High Seat (1995 ft/608m)** **Bleaberry Fell (1936ft/590m)** **Walla Crag (1243ft/379m)** **The shorter version visits only the summit of Walla Crag**
Start	**Great Wood**
Distance	**7.5 miles/12km**
Height gain	**2020ft/620m**
Time	**5.75 hours**
Map	**OS Explorer OL4 (North-western)**
Facilities	**In Keswick; the nearest toilets are adjacent to the Lakeside car park**

These figures reduce to 4.25 miles/6.75km, 980ft/300m and 3 hours if the shorter option is taken.

Parking: Park in the National Trust pay and display car park in Great Wood (NY 272214), which is 1.5 miles/2.5km south of Keswick on the Borrowdale Valley road (B5289).

The walk

Leave the car park southwards on a clear path which climbs gently into the wood. Go round a wooden barrier and continue straight on, ignoring all tracks going off left or right.

Approaching Cat Gill, keep right to cross the wooden footbridge, and follow the path as it swings right and drops down. The path continues high above Derwentwater, and excellent views of the lake, and of Catbells and Castle Crag beyond it, open up. The path undulates beneath Falcon Crag before arriving at a fork with a National Trust sign. Here keep left (signed Ashness Bridge) and continue on the easy path, which goes through a gate and drops onto a tarmac road just below Ashness Bridge.

Turn left, cross the bridge, and immediately over it (and having taken the obligatory photograph) leave the road on the left to climb gently the initially paved way with the stream on your left. Quickly meet a path coming in from the right besides the wall and swing left to continue uphill and cross a step-stile in a fence. 90yds further on there is a crosspaths; here the longer and shorter walks go different ways.

The shorter option

At the crosspaths, go left to the wooden footbridge over Ashness Gill. Cross the bridge and go straight on uphill, ignoring a wide path rising up from the road on the other side of the gill; this would have been a slightly shorter but distinctly less good alternative route. Continue to a small gate and go through, ignoring a second small gate on the left which is the end of a short-cut up from the Great Wood path. The clear, broad path then climbs gently, contouring round the head of Cat Gill and then heading towards a wall which has trees behind it and, to the right of the trees, the top of Walla Crag. The path coming down from the top of Bleaberry Fell, which is the longer walk, joins from the right at a cairn. Continue ahead, skipping forward in the text to the combined return.

The full walk

At the crosspaths, continue straight on to climb steeply on the increasingly grassy way with Ashness Gill over on the left, a wall (which

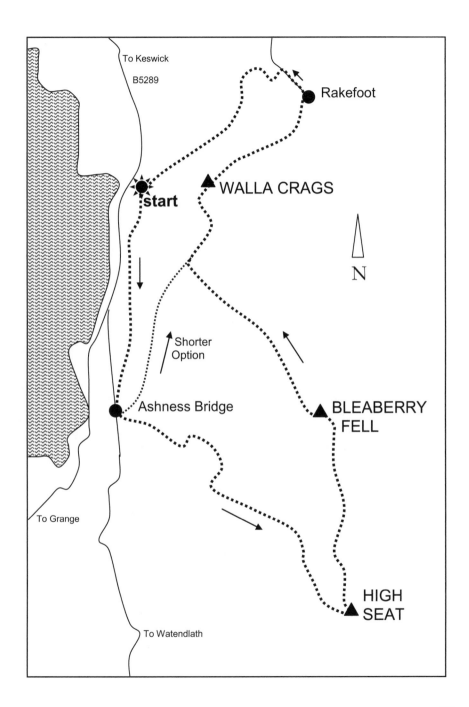

To Keswick

B5289

Rakefoot

start

WALLA CRAGS

N

Shorter
Option

Ashness Bridge

BLEABERRY
FELL

To Grange

HIGH
SEAT

To Watendlath

Derwentwater and Bassenthwaite Lake from above Cat Gill

becomes a fence at a solitary tree) on the right, and an expanding view of Derwentwater, Bassenthwaite and the north-western fells beyond Catbells behind. The gradient finally eases on reaching a kissing gate in a cross-wall. Go through, following the path which picks its way between boulders as it swings left to pass above a solitary tree and climbs gently round the hillside to return to within a few paces of Ashness Gill. Here the path swings right to climb briefly beside the stream before swinging right again to zig-zag up a stepped section to reach a big cairn on the crest of the ridge.

Here ignore the path going left, and that going right two paces further on, and go straight ahead on a path which immediately does a clear left turn. The path continues, ignoring a number of cairns on high points – which may well be mistaken for the summit of the fell, and heads on towards a high-point on the far horizon – which really is the top of High Seat. This section of the walk is likely to be wet, and, after inclement weather, may be unpleasantly so. An improvement finally comes on crossing the remains of a broken wall close to the foot of the final rise to the summit, on which you will find a large cairn and an Ordnance Survey column bearing the number S5987.

The view from the summit is excellent. Eastwards (ahead, as you arrive), beyond a fence running along the ridge, is another high point, named Man, which looks just as high as this one, and beyond that the whole of the Helvellyn ridge, with a small section of Thirlmere down half-right; north and south (left and right) the fence runs away along the broad ridge; and behind is the most glorious panorama sweeping round from the Scafells in the south-west, with the green swathe of the Seathwaite valley superbly displayed at their foot, through the north-western fells (with the sea beyond) to the Skiddaw massif in the north.

The short excursion to Man, to complete the visit to High Seat, is facilitated by a path leading to a step stile in the fence; there is little more to see in the view from here except a glimpse of the A591 besides Thirlmere, but it would be a shame to miss it.

Our return route over Bleaberry Fell also leaves the Ordnance Survey column eastwards on the path towards the fence but quickly, before reaching the fence, swings northwards to drop down and go over a little rocky knoll. As you go over the rocky knoll, ahead and below you can see the path going on along the ridge, running parallel to the fence and around 80yds away from it. Drop down off the rocky knoll a little awkwardly and then down a grass slope, heading north on the path which is making a bee-line for Bleaberry Fell – the high point on the skyline ahead, on which a cairn can just about be discerned. At the foot of the slope down from High Seat, at an area strangely named Threefooted Brandreth, wetter ground is rejoined, but it is not as all pervading as on the ascent. Mostly the path is extremely clear, but in places it disappears temporarily in wet ground. Shortly arrive at a good wire mesh cross-fence and cross the step stile.

The onward way is a pleasant and interesting wander along the good ridge path, with detours round half a dozen wet bits. At the foot of the rise to Bleaberry Fell, the wetness is left behind. At a fork, the right-hand way is the wider and more walked but both are good and grassy and rejoin close to the top of the fell. The path then passes a large cairn, and 50yds later arrives at the top of Bleaberry Fell. There is a large shelter and another wonderful view, which includes Blencathra, Skiddaw, the north-western hills, which are excellently displayed, and Scafell Pike.

Leave the top north-westwards on the very clear path, with an improving view of Derwentwater, heading towards the large cairn in the direction of Bassenthwaite Lake. The path drops to another large cairn where it turns left to descend stonily but easily; the onward path can now be seen running below round to the right towards Walla Crags. The way continues down stone steps and then, as the gradient eases, as a made path. Past some ruins on the left the surfacing finishes and the way continues to descend easily on grass and peat before becoming intermittent as it crosses an extensive wet area. The top of Walla Crag is now clearly visible ahead to the right of an area of trees. In the depression the path crosses two small streams, the second by a solitary tree, and then climbs slightly to a cairn where the direct path from Ashness Bridge comes in from the left. Turn right.

Combined return

Approaching a wall with trees beyond, go one way or the other to join the path coming in from the left, cross a step stile, and continue to the cairn on the rocky top of Walla Crags. This is not so much a mountain in its own right but the point on the slope down from Bleaberry Fell where the easy gradients end and the ground drops precipitously to Derwentwater.

There is a dramatic view of the lake, Borrowdale, the north-western fells (with Catbells pre-eminent), and Bassenthwaite.

Leave the summit, continuing in the same direction, on the narrow stony path. The way is only briefly steep, and then wanders gradually down to a kissing gate in the wall. Go through and turn left.

Continue gently downhill on the wide grassy path which runs along above the wall before descending more steeply and then swinging left with the wall to drop, now on a stony track, through a gate to a footbridge. Cross the bridge and go left on the tarmac lane. Keep left at a road junction and in a further 130yds go sharp left down a footpath (signed Keswick and Great Wood). Go through a gate, cross a small wooden footbridge and turn right as directed by the waymark. At a fork keep right to walk high above the stream. Go through a kissing gate and shortly go left at a finger-post (signed Great Wood and Borrowdale) and walk the almost level path with grand views to Catbells and the hills beyond.

The path enters Great Wood and drops slightly to cross a small stream, and then gently rises again. 15yds beyond the stream, go right on a narrow path which descends on grass. In a further 15yds, this narrow path joins a wide track coming in from the left and continues downhill with it. Follow the stony track down, continuing ahead where a track comes in from the right at a junction with a large tree. At a right–hand corner, beyond which the track levels in grassy surroundings and runs to a wooden vehicle barrier, take the narrow but clear path which goes off left from the corner. This takes you, in one minute, to the car park.

Walk 6
A Borrowdale exploration

Borrowdale is a beautiful valley, the joys of which can only be fully discovered in the course of numerous visits. Here, however, is a walk which explores many of its delights – and all without setting a foot on a motor road. The first part of the route takes in riverside and woodland (including Wainwright's loveliest square mile in Lakeland), whilst the return is made along the crest of one of the valley's enclosing ridges and through the remains of its mining past. The walk also visits Peace How, a beautiful, tranquil spot, well deserving of its name, as well as offering the option of a detour to the less tranquil but equally beautiful, summit of Catbells.

Summits visited	**Maiden Moor (1890ft/576m)** **High Spy (2143ft/653m)**
Start	**Rosthwaite**
Distance	**8.5 miles/13.75km**
Height gain	**2050ft/620m**
Time	**5.5 hours**
Map	**OS Explorer OL4 (North-western)**
Facilities	**There are toilets adjacent to the National Trust car park, and two hotels in the village. The Flock-In Tea Room, 100yds from the car park, is passed on both outward and return legs of the walk, but was closed on Wednesdays at the time of writing**

Parking: Just to the north of the narrow section of the B5289 in Rosthwaite, a narrow lane running west leads to a National Trust Car Park (NY 257148). A small amount of additional parking is also available immediately beyond this by the Village Hall. If this is all full, the Scafell Hotel, which is on the main road on the southern side of the village, permits parking on its car park by non-patrons on payment of a fee at the Hotel Reception.

The walk

Walk up the tarmac lane away from main road, pass the Flock-In Tea Room and bear right between the buildings of Yew Tree Farm. Follow the rough track round to the right to follow the River Derwent to a stone arched bridge. Cross it and turn right to two gates side by side. Go through the right hand one (which has an accompanying stile) and follow the track by the river. At the fork, go left away from the river and continue on the level main track. Pass three large cairns and go through a gap in a wall, ignoring minor paths off to the left, and climb past a spoil heap to a three-way junction. Take the middle way and climb to a finger post, here turning right, signposted Grange.

The path descends through a gap in a wall, shortly to return to the river bank and pass through a gate/stile. Ignore the path to Honister going off uphill left, cross two footbridges and continue ahead on the broad path into the campsite, keeping right alongside the wall.

Where the track forks, go left and keep left on the tarmac lane to pass through Hollows Farm and continue on the clear track beyond. Through a gate the path swings right, drops slightly and then climbs gently to approach a stone wall in which is a gate marked private. Here our way goes left, but first take a 100yd detour through the waymarked gate on the right to visit Peace How, which is not named on the OS 1:25000 map. Through the gate, ignore the little path going right and go straight ahead up the short grass slope and then left a few paces to arrive at a slate bench in a beautiful location overlooking Grange Village and with a view to Castle Crag. The bench is inscribed "This property was presented to the National Trust by Canon Rawnsley, in 1917".

Return through the waymarked gate and continue ahead parallel to the wall on the right on a less distinct path which climbs the gentle slope. Just over the brow, climb a step stile and go right to quickly cross a footbridge. The path continues on a gently rising course to pass just above a light coloured rocky outcrop. Beyond, Derwentwater, Skiddaw and Blencathra appear ahead as the path now descends slightly to cross some

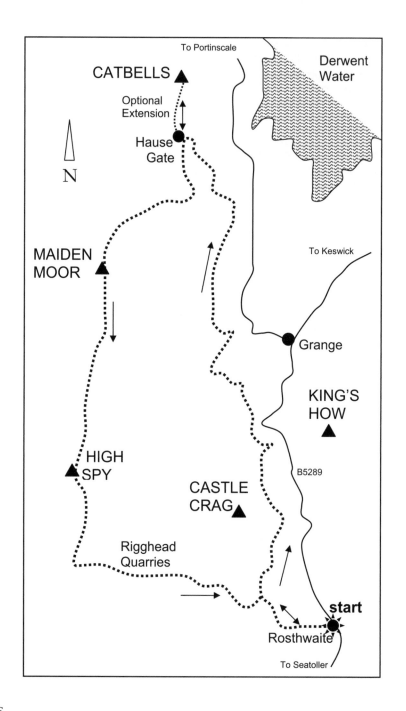

boggy patches and then run above a small coniferous plantation, just beyond which is a fork. Go left uphill and soon our way up to the skyline is revealed. Join the major path coming up from the right, keeping left at the fork to continue climbing on the recently repaired path to reach the ridge at Hause Gate, the col between Catbells and Maiden Moor.

Here the main path goes right to the summit of Catbells (to which a detour, adding 0.75 miles/1.25km and 300ft/90m of ascent to the walk, may be made), but we continue ahead to meet the ridge path at the col itself, which is marked with a small cairn. Turn left and follow the clear path up Maiden Moor. Where the ground levels, leave the main path on a thinner trod which goes round the far side of a rocky knoll on the right; this junction is marked by a number of small cairns but is easily missed. This thinner path runs to a cairn with a good view northwards, and then round the edge of the plateau to visit the summit cairn on Maiden Moor, from which there are excellent views into and across the Newlands Valley. (The main path runs across the flank of the hill to cut off the corner, but misses both the view and the summit.) Continue from the summit, and shortly rejoin the main path. Ahead is a ridge at the left hand end of which is a prominent cairn. This is Blea Crag and is well worth the short detour from the well-cairned junction for the excellent view of Derwentwater. Return to the main path and follow it as it wanders on a fairly level course for a further half mile to the impressive summit cairn on High Spy.

[In poor weather it is recommended to continue ahead on the main path, which keeps close to the edge above Newlands, and follow it down into the depression; then, beyond where it is joined by the path rising from Newlands, and close to the tarn, find a trod heading left (east) across marshy ground to a stile and the return path down through the quarries.]

Otherwise, leave the summit half-left to walk south of south east on a faint path to a prominent cairn – which becomes clearly visible on the near skyline on crossing an intervening low rise. Beyond the cairn, the faint onward path can be seen running due south before swinging right and becoming clearer as it heads south west, following a line towards a distant tarn. The path descends easily on grass and arrives at a cross-paths where there is a low flat heap of slate and a slate cairn. Go left, and shortly swing right to descend on grass and cross a stile in a fence.

Descending through Rigghead Quarries

Advance to a big heap of stones and swing left on a clear path which descends, mostly on steps, through the disused Rigghead Quarries.

Below the old workings cross a stile and continue down, keeping Tongue Gill on the left. Then, approaching the intake wall, cross a major path and continue ahead to a gate. Go through and escape from unpleasant stones onto a grassy path on the right. After ignoring a ladder stile on the right the path fades, but continue ahead towards the village below, picking up the reappearing path which swings right and runs down into the valley to cross a stile in the far right-hand corner of the field by the river. Cross two wooden footbridges, doing a dog-leg right on leaving the second to go through what used to be a kissing gate, and follow the grassy way. Cross a stile, go left, cross another wooden footbridge and almost immediately turn right over the stone arched bridge to retrace steps to the village.

Walk 7
Blencathra

The distinctive and attractive profile of Blencathra is a familiar sight in many views in the north of the region, and dominates the approach to Lakeland from the east along the A66. It is very much a mountain which demands to be climbed, and one which provides routes for every taste. Its dramatic southern face, consisting of a series of scree gullies and rocky edges, provides mountaineering experiences which rank with the best in the region. Its other aspects, however, consist mostly of simple grassy slopes which cater admirably for those seeking more pedestrian approaches. This walk of course uses only the easy slopes; an ascent from the west via Blease Fell leads to a full traverse of the mountain's long top, which provides, from secure terrain, good views of its wilder edges and ravines. The northern return, over the hump of Mungrisdale Common and along the deep Glenderaterra valley between Blencathra and the Skiddaw massif, includes a pathless three-quarters of a mile.

Summits visited	**Blencathra (2847ft/868m)** **Mungrisdale Common (2077ft/633m)**
Start	**Blencathra Centre**
Distance	**6.75 miles/10.75km**
Height gain	**2280ft/690m**
Time	**5 hours**
Map	**OS Explorer OL4 (North-western) and OL5 (North-eastern)**
Facilities	**In Threlkeld, there are (signposted) toilets on the car park behind the Public Rooms. The village also has a post office/shop, with limited opening, and two Inns**

Parking: Use the parking area by the Blencathra Centre (NY 302256). Driving eastwards through Threlkeld Village, turn left up "Blease Road leading to Blencathra". In just over a mile, where the tarmac ends, keep right at the fork (left goes into the Blencathra Centre) and in a few tens of yards find a parking area for a dozen and a half vehicles.

The walk

Leave the parking area using the grassy path (signed Blencathra) which climbs diagonally right across the hillside. Shortly, approaching a low crag, a number of paths converge; go left and follow this grass path as it climbs diagonally left to rise above the valley of Glenderaterra Beck, with Latrigg and Lonscale Fell opposite. The path turns right and, now less distinct but still easy to follow, climbs some little zig-zags. The gradient soon eases and the path arrives at a T-junction; turn left onto the broad stony way and climb a number of small zig-zags. Depending on whether you are zigging or zagging, in view ahead is the Skiddaw massif (going left) or the Helvellyn ridge (going right). Above the zig-zags the path continues to rise easily to a high point where the way ahead to the top of Blencathra comes into view. The path now drops slightly and swings round the impressive rocky coomb of Knowe Crags before climbing to the subsidiary summit of Gategill Fell Top, from which it is a simple but splendid short walk round the rim of the crags to the summit of Blencathra (Hallsfell Top).

From here there is a good view of the crags alongside our route of arrival, and of the more challenging path directly climbing the ridge of Hall's Fell. Beyond, the majority of the high mountains of Lakeland are well displayed in a broad southern arc from the Pennines round to Skiddaw. There is no OS column but, unusually, a concrete ring on the ground inscribed "Ordnance Survey Trigonometric Station".

Leave the summit northwards on a faint path which runs across the so-called saddle (which gives the mountain its alternative but much less attractive name of Saddleback) towards a conspicuous white object and three prominent cairns. After a few paces a small tarn appears in the depression; the path goes to the right of this, climbs to the first cairn, and approaches the white object, which turns out to be a cross made out of white stones laid on the ground. Beyond the cross, the path continues to the second and then the third of the cairns, which marks the top of Foule Crag from where there is an extensive view northwards.

A few yards further on, at a smaller pile of stones, a path will be found which drops down stony zig-zags on the left and can be seen continuing on a long way, diverging in the distance to run to Bannerdale Crags (right fork) or to Bowscale Fell (left fork). Take this path down to the bottom of the stony slope where the gradient eases and the path swings right. Here there is a walled construction (a sort of rough two sided shelter), and, some 30-40yds further on, beyond a little depression, a small rocky knoll. From the centre of this little depression leave the path at a right-angle on the left to walk north-westwards. There is no path initially but one is quickly found which runs to the highest point of the gently swelling ground ahead – which is the top of Mungrisdale Common. Follow this thin grassy trod to find a small neat pile of stones marking the summit – although the highest point could actually be anywhere hereabouts.

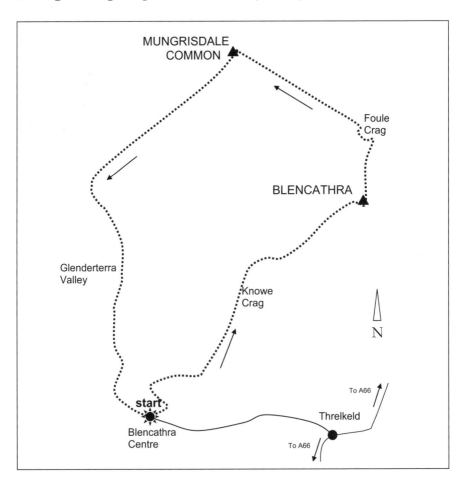

Looking back along the edge of the summit plateau

From here radiate many thin paths. Take the one running south-west and heading towards a little lump on the near horizon. At bifurcations keep left maintaining the south-west course and heading towards the summit of Lonscale Fell, some 2 miles/3.25km distant across the valley of Glenderaterra Beck. When, in due course, the track peters out, maintain the same direction. An elegant cairn may be seen on the right, but this, and any other piles of stones spotted nearby, are of no particular navigational help. Eventually, the valley of the Glenderaterra appears ahead and the developing gash of Sinen Gill is seen on the left.

Three walled enclosures come into view across the valley. Keeping Sinen Gill on the left, head for the lower left hand corner of these enclosures. Here a very clear path will be found descending by the wall to cross the Glenderaterra. Turn left onto this and cross the plank bridge over Sinen Gill. Continue on the good track which runs down the valley on a virtually level course and in 1.5 miles/2.5km arrives directly back at the parking area.

Walk 8
The Caldbeck Fells

Tucked away at the very north of the National Park, between the Skiddaw/Blencathra massif to the south and the coastal plain of the Solway to the north, is an area of grassy hills, five of which overtop 2000ft/600m, known locally as 'Back o' Skidda'. This walk explores this quiet area of rolling uplands. The terrain could hardly be described as exciting, but does provide easy walking on which miles can be covered relatively quickly. Being close to the edge of the higher ground, the views to the coast, to the Pennines and into Scotland, provide excellent panoramas of distant hills and water. In mist, a paucity of landmarks could make this a tricky route to follow if unfamiliar with the geography.

Summits visited	**High Pike (2157ft/657m)** **Knott (2329ft/710m)** **Great Sca Fell (2136ft/651m)** **Brae Fell (1923ft/586m)**
Start	**Fell Side**
Distance	**8.75 miles/14km**
Height gain	**2060ft/630m**
Time	**5 hours**
Map	**OS Explorer OL4 (North-western) and OL5 (North-eastern)**
Facilities	**Caldbeck is 2 miles/3.25km away and has a general store, cafés, a pub, toilets and fuel. John Peel, of hunting song fame, is buried in its churchyard**

Parking: Park at Fell Side (NY 304374). Approaching from the west through Green Head and Branthwaite, take the first opening on the right after entering the hamlet; from the Caldbeck direction, turn left into the wide

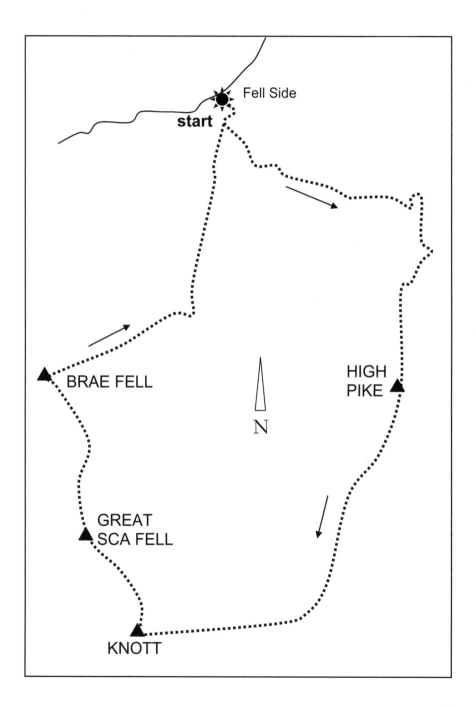

Fell Side

start

BRAE FELL

HIGH PIKE

N

GREAT
SCA FELL

KNOTT

space approaching the end of the hamlet. Go up past the postbox and Fellside Farm, just above which there is space to park around ten cars.

The walk

From the parking area, walk up the track. Go through the gate and follow the rough track round to the right past an information board, following a wall-sign (Roughten Gill & Caldbeck Fells) and a finger-post (Calebreck). After 80yds, at a blue Public Bridleway waymark arrow, turn left up a wide grassy track. After around 250yds, there is a fork with tracks continuing either side of a low mound; take the clearer and slightly steeper right-hand branch. Just before the track reaches a brow, over which it starts to fall slightly, there is a second fork; here take the left-hand path, which although initially less clear, can be seen running through the heather ahead. Follow this as it climbs gently to a T-junction. Here go left on the stony track which descends gently to the site of the old Potts Gill mine, where it swings left to cross Potts Gill and then right at an open area which is the top of a spoil heap. A few yards further a clear path goes off right up the fellside. Follow this as it climbs steadily, parallel to the gill, up towards another old spoil heap.

As the now narrower way passes most closely to the spoil heap, a junction is reached. A faintish trod comes in uphill from the right, and the way we have been travelling continues on less distinctly ahead, but the most clear way comes in from the left and goes off half right. Take the path going half right, and follow it as it runs across above the spoil heap, and then swings left uphill and immediately right before rising gently for a couple of minutes to a little brow where a small pile of stones marks a junction with a cross-path. Here go left uphill and follow the path to shortly pass a large shelter and arrive at the OS column on the summit of High Pike. A fine slate seat nearby provides an excellent resting place to admire the extensive view of Skiddaw and Blencathra, the Cumbrian coast, the Scottish hills beyond the Solway, and the Pennines.

From the summit, continue in the same direction on a clear path heading south, and to the left of the top of Knott, which is our next objective. In the depression turn right onto the clear stony track, and follow it along the broad ridge to pass some fenced enclosures on the right and the hut on Great Lingy Hill. The path descends into a boggy hollow where the main path (which is the Cumbria Way) trends left to go down to Mosedale. Our way however continues straight on to cross the stream, beyond which

The hut on Great Lingy Hill

the onward path can be seen (slightly right) ascending a grassy bank to the skyline. So, pick a way across the marshy ground, keeping an eye on the path on the far bank, cross the stream (Grainsgill Beck) easily, and climb the clear steep path towards the skyline. The gradient soon eases, and the path swings right to continue easily to the grassy top of Knott, the highest point on the walk.

Leave the summit on the path heading north-west and the way ahead soon becomes clear. The path swings right to cross a shallow depression and then climbs to the cairn on Great Sca Fell, from which Bassenthwaite Lake is now in view. The path continues across a second depression and rises over the cairned top of Little Sca Fell, before continuing north across a further depression to the large cairn on Brae Fell, at which another amazingly expansive view awaits.

Leave the top of Brae Fell with the little shelter on your left to follow the clear path running north-east. In theory, a direct return to the car is possible by continuing down this path to a ford across Dale Beck. However, the ford is only crossable dry-shod in wellingtons (and an alternative unauthorised crossing via the top of a sheep barrier is not recommended). Therefore, in order to complete the walk with dry feet, a detour to a footbridge a little higher up Dale Beck is required.

To take this detour, note shortly (150yds) after leaving the summit, a ravine which appears ahead, to the right of where the path appears to go; this is Ramps Gill. We are going to leave the path at some point to walk to the right of the top of Ramps Gill to reach the high point on the fell boundary to the right of it. So carry on down the path to where the gradient eases a bit, the path swings left to go round a marshy area with two water filled holes/puddles, and the ground begins to get humpy and furrowed. Here strike off right and walk eastwards toward the high point of the fell boundary. This is pathless but easy, dry walking.

Continue over the high point on the edge of the summit plateau, and as the downward slope of the ground steepens, find one or more of the furrows which run down the hillside and quickly become two clear parallel grassy gulleys. Walk down beside either on steep but otherwise pleasant easy turf, noting the view up to the old mine workings at the head of Roughten Gill. Continue down to the clearly visible green valley path which runs along above the stream, and turn left onto it. Descend to and cross the footbridge, then going left to follow the good track which runs round the hillside. This passes some areas of newly planted trees, and eventually turns left to go through the gate above the parking area.

Walk 9
Skiddaw

You may well meet walkers who dismiss Skiddaw as dull or second rate. Take no notice; Skiddaw is a fine mountain – one of only four in Lakeland which overtop 3000ft, and a splendid backdrop to many views of Derwentwater. Described here is a route which, in virtually every way, is hugely to be preferred to the popular and busy return trip from the environs of Keswick, and indeed is as good a day on the summits of Lakeland as most. Its one disadvantage is that the start of the walk is more out of way and has more limited parking than the popular routes.

Summits visited	Ullock Pike (2230ft/680m) Long Side (2405ft/734m) Carl Side (2447ft/746m) Skiddaw (3053ft/931m)
Start	High Side, south of Bassenthwaite village
Distance	7 miles/11.25km
Height gain	3020ft/920m
Time	6 hours
Map	OS Explorer OL4 (North-western)
Facilities	The nearest refreshments and toilets are at the Forest Enterprise car park at Dodd Wood on the A591, just short of 2 miles/3km towards Keswick

Parking: At High Side, just over 5.5 miles/9km north of Keswick on the A591, a minor road forks off right to Orthwaite. Around 400yds along this road, there is a parking space with room for half a dozen cars (NY 236310). Unfortunately, if this space is full there is not really a realistic alternative. Two parking spaces further up the lane adjacent to Peter House Farm, are a full mile distant.

The walk

A few yards up the lane from the parking space is a gate with a Public Bridleway sign. Go through and follow the track past a sign to Skiddaw, and across a stream. The track bears right to climb gently alongside gorse, above which Ullock Pike, our first objective, dominates the skyline. At a waymark, turn right to walk in front of a single line of hawthorns, continuing beyond the end of the trees on a grass path which swings left to climb to a waymarked gate/ladder stile. Go through this and then a second gate/ladder stile at the top of the field. The onward wide grass path initially continues ahead towards Skiddaw, but then swings right to head directly towards Ullock Pike and reach a gate/stile in the intake wall. Go through and immediately turn right off the track (which is our return route) up the path by the wall. This soon fades, but continue the short distance onto the crest of the ridge and bend left to climb up the ridge end opposite a small gate.

There is initially only a suggestion of a path but the way rapidly becomes clearer as it winds along the top of the ridge, heading directly for Ullock Pike. Beyond a minor dip, continue ahead at a crosspaths to climb to the right of a small crag and arrive at the Watches, a high point with a cairn and a jumble of rocks. From here, drop into a depression, where paths join both from the right and the left, and then tackle the excellent climb up The Edge. The pleasant path wanders up the ridge, climbing sometimes to the left and sometimes to the right of its crest, and leads to a final short, steep section which is eroded, but has no difficulties.

The summit of Ullock Pike is small and pointy, and has an excellent view. Perhaps most striking in the panorama is the full length of Bassenthwaite with the Solway, Criffel and plenty of wind turbines beyond. Across the lake is Lord's Seat, and then looking round to the south are Grisedale Pike, Thornthwaite, Braithwaite, the Newlands Valley, Keswick, Derwentwater and then pretty much the whole of the rest of Lakeland.

Take the only possible route off the summit, the path running the short distance along the neat ridge to Long Side. During this easy traverse, note on the left the clear line running across the scree and up onto the summit ridge of Skiddaw – this is our route to the top. The summit of Long Side is unremarkable; it has a little pile of stones, but the path doesn't even bother to detour a few metres to visit it, preferring to pass by on its right-hand side and continue down to the col, where there is a fork. The major path goes left and climbs round the flank of Carl Side, whilst a smaller, more pleasant path forks right and climbs the short distance to its top. As visiting the summit involves little extra height gain and loss, take the

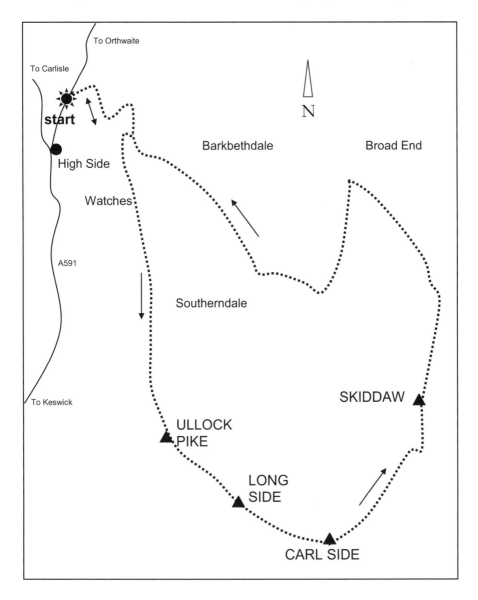

pleasanter right-hand path and continue to the cairn on the summit of Carl Side. Here our path meets the major route coming up from Millbeck and we turn left onto it and drop into the sometimes wet depression between Carl Side and Skiddaw, continuing ahead past the diminutive Carlside tarn. Here the direct path joins from the left and we begin the final ascent up what looks like a horrible path. In fact the climb is nothing like as bad as it looks, with the exception of one short, steeper section. As the gradient eases and the crest of the ridge is reached at a large shelter, we join the crowds on the "tourist path" from Keswick and turn left with them to walk the short distance to the summit of Skiddaw, where there is another shelter, a triangulation column and a view indicator.

Leave the summit continuing in the same direction (north), towards two large piles of stones/shelters. At the second, the ground begins to fall away more steeply towards Broad End. Descend the stony path easily to a shallow depression, where the path ends abruptly by a cairn at the foot of the slope, with the grassy hump of Broad End ahead and to the left. (Just before the bottom of the slope there is a flat cairn to the left of the path. If you step left to the edge here and look over you will see below, at the foot of a scree slope, a sledgate running down Barkbethdale. Our return route goes down this sledgate, but to reach it we are going to do a loop round to the right to circumvent the scree.)

From the cairn at the end of the path, set off half-left (between north and north-west) towards a prominent cairn. Continue in the same direction, to walk over, or near to, the highest point of Broad End just ahead to reach another cairn. Continue again in the same direction and in 10 or 12 paces another cairn appears a little to the right. Pass this, and after a few further paces, look around for three smallish cairns which mark the beginning of an obvious path going down. (Between the end of the main path which dropped from the summit, and the beginning of the descent path at the three cairns is around 300yds.)

Proceed downhill on the developing path, avoiding stony sections by detouring onto the plentiful grass. Soon the path ahead appears running clearly below. Continue dropping down, and in due course, over on the left, the sledgate down Barkbethdale appears, still some way below us. Carry on down on steepish grass, and shortly after passing an area of white stones on the left, a very clear cross-path appears below. Turn left onto this narrow but well-trodden path and follow it as it cuts back across

The Skiddaw massif from the north; the walk traverses the skyline from right to left, and descends the broad shoulder of Broad End

the top of Barkbethdale, winding through the heather and falling a little to reach the top of the sledgate.

Walk down the gently graded, grassy way, passing a big white boulder by the side of the path and a sheepfold down on the right. Then, shortly, just beyond a shallow, dry gully, leave the sledgate at a clear fork, going left on the thin, clear path which rises gently up the side of the ridge and then swings left to reach its crest. Here the Ullock Pike ridge appears across Southerndale. Turn right and follow the narrow, sometimes vague, path which initially keeps to the top of the ridge and then begins to descend its left-hand flank. Here note, down on the left, a track rising from the beck on the far side of Southerndale and heading off down the valley; this is our onward route. Ignore a thin cross-path and keep left as the way very clearly starts to descend to the bridge across the beck. Two good paths join from the right and we arrive at the sleeper bridge which crosses Southerndale Beck adjacent to an interestingly shaped sheepfold. Follow the clear track which swings right and runs down the valley to the gate in the intake wall through which we arrived. Go through and follow the track as it swings left to retrace steps to the parking area.

Walk 10
Loughrigg

Loughrigg Fell is not high. It can be climbed easily and quickly, and it rewards with excellent views, not only from its summit, but also from numerous points on its slopes and extensive top. However, despite its modest altitude, it is not a straightforward hill; its top is no neat dome, but a mile-long sprawling upland with a veritable labyrinth of paths and many false "summits". The walk described provides an interesting and straightforward circular route which visits all the best places on the fell.

Summit visited	Loughrigg Fell (1101ft/335m)
Start	White Moss Common
Distance	5.75 miles/9.25km
Height gain	1220ft/370m
Time	3.75 hours
Map	OS Explorer OL7 (South-eastern)
Facilities	There are toilets at White Moss between the lower car park and the footbridge. An ice cream van reliably parks adjacent to the upper parking area. Grasmere has shops, accommodation and many eating places

Parking: On the A591 at White Moss Common, 1 mile/1.5km north of Rydal village, there are two National Park Authority pay and display car parks (NY 350065). Driving north, there is a "lower" car park on the left, and a little further on, an "upper" car park on the right.

[An alternative plan (if making an early start) is to park on the small car park near Pelter Bridge, NY 364059, referred to at the end of the third paragraph. This is reached from the A591 by crossing the narrow bridge over the River Rothay 300yds south of Rydal village and then turning immediately right over a cattle grid. The parking area is a further 250yds on the left. Returning here from the walk, go right at the waymarked fork on Loughrigg Terrace, which provides a virtually level route to Rydal Cave.]

The walk

From the lower car park: In the corner diagonally opposite the entry ramp there is a vehicle barrier from which a track runs parallel to the river to reach a footbridge over it. There are toilets on the right shortly after leaving the car park and before crossing the stream. **From the upper car park:** Leave by the main vehicle entry, cross the road, go through the gap in the wall and follow the path down (or detour left to the toilets). On reaching the broad track which runs parallel to the River Rothay, go right to the footbridge.

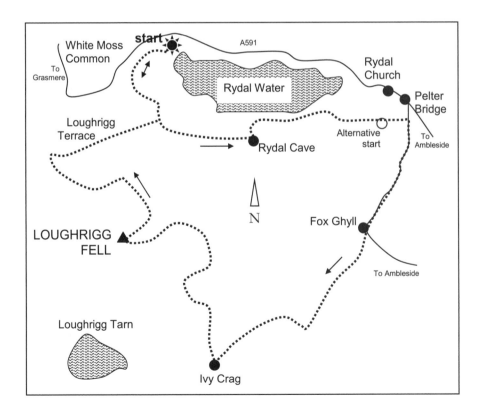

Cross the footbridge, leaving it slightly right on the wide path (signed Loughrigg Terrace and Rydal Lake) which climbs through the wood to a gate in a wall. Go through and continue ahead on a path (signed Steps End via Rydal Cave) which rises a little and then contours left. Cross the flat top of an old slate spoil heap to reach Rydal Cave – a cavernous hole which was formerly a part of Loughrigg Quarry. Exploration of the cave's outer parts is possible but strongly discouraged.

Continue on the wide track which zig-zags downhill, passes more old quarry workings, crosses a stream and then descends to run a level course above Rydal Lake. Stay on the top path rather than dropping to the lakeside and continue to a gate. Go through and continue above the wall. The way becomes walled on both sides and beyond another gate becomes a surfaced lane which passes a small parking area.

Continue down the lane, cross the cattle grid and at the T-junction turn right to walk along in company with the River Rothay. In a little over half a mile, just before you reach Foxghyll, a large white Guest House, go up a few stone steps on the right and through a kissing gate (signed Loughrigg Fell). The path climbs to a metal kissing gate, descends some steps to cross a wooden footbridge and then climbs steeply through some rhododendrons. The gradient eases as the path emerges from the bushes, and continues up a shallow valley, firstly with a stream and then with a wall on the left. Shortly, come over a rise and see the wall doing a left-hand turn and, a similar distance ahead, a small pointy mound. Before reaching the wall corner and mound, find a fork where a thin grassy trod branches off right. Take this less distinct right-hand branch, continuing in the same direction where it briefly fades, now with the mound on the left, to shortly meet a clear path. Continue straight ahead across this (rather than turning right along it), quickly go over a small rise and follow the path across the damp depression ahead where it crosses a significant path and bends very slightly right. Go over a second small rise to where a stream crosses our route. Two paths go on from the stream; eventually all ways join, but take the right hand one. Approaching a rocky tor, join a path coming in from the left and keep right to climb round the right-hand side of the tor on a path which curves round left and joins a major route which seems to have come over the tor. Go right and continue to climb.

Where the path levels out, fork left on a narrow path and continue ahead across a broad path to walk gently uphill up a shallow valley. The path becomes very faint, but continue in the same direction and shortly arrive at a T-junction from where you will see the cairn on Ivy Crag half-left. Turn left and go to it. From here there is a decent view of Windermere to the left and a bird's eye view of Skelwith Bridge below; there is also a view of the head of the Langdale valley but an intervening spur hides some of it.

From the cairn, return the way you arrived; the path is heading towards the top of Loughrigg, which is the distant flat bit on the skyline, but 20 paces beyond the T-junction where you arrived from the right, detour left along the spur for a far superior view of the Langdale and Coniston Fells with Loughrigg tarn in the foreground. Return to the path heading for the summit which passes a large cairn on its right and drops slightly to re-join the major path. Go left on it, pass the top of a good path coming up from Skelwith Bridge and ignore a level, greener path running off right. Wind a bit left uphill on what is obviously the main path. There is a narrower clear path going up left to a little height with a cairn on top; this is Wainwright's recommended viewpoint for Loughrigg tarn and is worth a look.

The main path arrives at a rise beyond which there is a wet depression with a small tarn. Here the main path swings left and drops into a significant dip, on the far side of which it can be seen climbing away towards the summit column. This would indeed take you to the top, but for a more pleasant journey which avoids the descent and re-ascent of the main path, fork right on the grassier path which drops only slightly and swings left round the back of the tarn to approach the summit from the east. Continue on this clear path which wanders through hummocky ground, ignoring all divergences left or right. Immediately beyond a small tarn in a hollow, briefly do a bit of more serious climbing to arrive at a many-way junction of paths. Here keep left to quickly find yourself on the summit plateau, 100yds from the Ordnance Survey column.

For a fell of such modest height, the view is surprisingly comprehensive in all directions.

Leave the top west of north, heading towards Grasmere village, where a clear path very quickly appears. This popular and mostly repaired route soon drops more steeply to arrive at a prominent cairn with an excellent view over Grasmere Lake to Helm Crag and Dunmail Raise. Here the path turns left and continues down uneventfully to arrive on a wide well-made path where you turn right to walk the gently descending, delightful Loughrigg Terrace. At the waymarked fork, keep left on the main path which continues to drop gently.

Looking over Grasmere on the descent to Loughrigg Terrace

On reaching a T-junction just in front of a wall, go right and follow the clear path down. Soon look for the gate in the wall on the left through which we came. Return through it and retrace your steps to the car at White Moss Common.

Walk 11
Little Langdale and Lingmoor Fell

Lingmoor Fell, although not of particularly great altitude, offers spectacular views of the head of Great Langdale. This interesting and easy circuit combines its ascent with a wander around Little Langdale with its quintessential whitewashed cottages and one of the prettiest bridges in Lakeland. Uniquely in the book, there is also a pub just about half way round. Side Pike can be omitted from the circuit, but shouldn't be. The last 1.5 miles/2.5km of the access road from Great Langdale is steep and/or narrow; all roads in Little Langdale are narrow.

Summits visited	**Lingmoor Fell (1539ft/469m)** **Side Pike (1187ft/362m)**
Start	**Blea Tarn**
Distance	**6.75 miles/10.75km**
Height gain	**1440ft/440m**
Time	**5 hours**
Map	**OS Explorer OL6 (South-western) and OL7 (South-eastern)**
Facilities	**The nearest facilities to the car park are at the Dungeon Ghyll Old Hotel in Great Langdale (refreshments and bar). Just over 2.75 miles/4.5km into the walk, the Three Shires Inn in Little Langdale makes an excellent lunch stop and lies only 300yd off route**

If Side Pike is omitted, the height gain is reduced by 200ft/70m and the time by 0.5 hours.

Parking: Park in the National Trust pay and display car park opposite Blea Tarn on the minor road between the head of Great Langdale and Little Langdale (NY 295043).

The walk

Unconventionally, the walk starts by heading downhill and directly away from our objective! So, cross the road, and walk down the broad path past the tarn. Cross a wooden footbridge, and immediately fork left to go through a kissing gate. The narrow path initially follows the stream but then drifts away from it to briefly descend alongside a wall. Where the wall bends away left, the path keeps straight on for 40yds to a rocky lump; here keep right and drop down to a small ruin. Then follow the path round the contour above the boggy area and continue ahead to climb the slope to the narrow tarmac road.

Turn left onto the road and follow it downhill. Just before it bends right to go past Fell Foot Farm, there is a kissing gate on the right which gives access to Ting Mound. This is a low mound enclosed by a fence which,

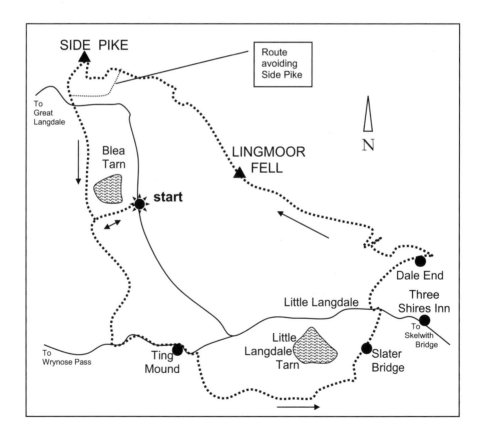

Bridge End with the slopes of Blake Rigg beyond

according to the National Trust sign, was used as an open air meeting place by courts and bodies responsible for the administration and organisation of the countryside.

Leave the mound by the same kissing gate and continue on the lane past the farm and round the left-hand corner beyond. Then in 70yds turn right off the road across the stone arched bridge over the River Brathy. Just over the bridge is a kissing gate on which is a small memorial plaque to Janet Laithwaite with the words "Her little legs took her far" – which is rather nice. Follow the track across the valley floor and over the bridge spanning Greenburn Beck at Bridge End. The track swings left and climbs gently. The water which appears on the left is Little Langdale Tarn, and the high ground beyond it is Lingmoor Fell.

Shortly after the miners' track from Greenburn joins from the right, go left at the fork and drop down the stony track. Enter a walled lane through a gate and continue down past High Hallgarth and Low Hallgarth, two typically Lakeland whitewashed cottages – both now National Trust holiday lets. Continue along the lane (from where, over on the left, our onward way can be seen clearly climbing a grass slope) and shortly go through a kissing gate in the wall on the left. Drop down to a step stile, go over and cross the ancient and very pretty Slater Bridge over the River Brathy. Then, having paused for photographs, and to admire the skills of the builders, climb the path with a wall on the right and at the top turn left onto the farm track and walk to the tarmac road.

Here turn right if you wish to visit the Three Shires Inn, but otherwise go left and then immediately right on Cycle Route 37 (signed Ambleside (challenging option)). Pass Dale End Farm, just beyond which the tarmac ends, and shortly leave the broad track on the left through a small gate by a field gate. Follow the path half left to go through two further gates and emerge on the fellside. The path swings right and zig-zags more steeply uphill. However, soon the gradient eases and the well engineered path swings left and wanders its way up the lengthy ridge. Where the way arrives at the foot of a slate heap, keep left on the main path round below the stones.

From here the way winds on most pleasantly along the grassy ridge and traverses two subsidiary summits with a significant depression between them. Beyond the second false summit, the ridge wall turns right; initially the path turns right with it but shortly swings left to resume the original direction of travel. Then, at a cairn around 40yds from the wall, a narrow stony path branches right up the slope; take this and tackle the short, sharp climb, preferring adjacent grass towards the top where the trodden way is badly eroded. Continue on the good path to pass a large cairn and then follow the line of the fence, and quickly arrive at, and climb, a stile adjacent to the summit rocks. The view of the Coniston Fells across Little Langdale is good, but the view of the mountains around the head of Great Langdale – notably the Pikes, Bowfell, Crinkle Crags and Pike o' Blisco – is magnificent, and arguably gets better on the descent.

Leave the top on the rocky path which continues alongside the wall/fence and descends two short, steeper sections without difficulty. However, it then arrives at the top of a longer and even steeper descent, from the top of which the path can be seen continuing below on the other side of the wall, having crossed it at an unseen stile. Here take the right-hand option which does a long, easy zig-zag to circumvent the steepness. Cross the stile and descend the grassy slope to the kissing-gate in the fence at the foot of Side Pike.

To omit Side Pike, do not cross the fence but go left alongside it to descend the pitched path. Cross the stile on the right and follow the path which runs parallel to and above the motor road. Go through the gap in the wall, leaving the small fenced enclosure leftwards and descending to the kissing gate which gives access to the road by the cattle grid, not far from our starting point. Skip ahead to the last paragraph.

To include Side Pike, go through the kissing-gate and follow the well-trodden path which initially climbs a little and then swings left and descends a little. Here you have to squeeze behind a big rock, which necessitates taking off your rucksack, but otherwise is straightforward. Beyond this there are just a few paces of slight exposure but they are quickly passed. Then simply follow the clear path, going right at a junction, the short distance to the top of Side Pike, where there is a pile of stones. This is a fine place to be; the aerial view of the head of Great Langdale is excellent.

Leave the top the same way as you arrived, heading westwards towards Crinkle Crags and the head of Oxendale. Retrace steps down to the junction, where go right to drop into the hollow. Ignoring various grassy paths going left, continue ahead on the obviously trodden way with the broken wall on the right. Traverse two rocky lumps, the second of which has a huge cairn, and pick a way down, guided by the sketchy path, and watching for where it crosses to the other side of the broken wall to avoid some low crags. Descend to a new kissing gate in a wire fence, and continue to a second kissing gate which gives access to the road not far from our starting point.

Cross the road by the cattle grid and continue on the well-made track which swings left through a gate and follow it back past Blea Tarn, turning left at the end of the water to cross the footbridge and retrace steps to the car park.

Walk 12
The classic Coniston round
– shorter version

The circuit from Coniston over the Old Man and Wetherlam, taking in Swirl How and Brim Fell on the way, has understandably become something of a classic. Its attractions, and accessibility, make it a popular destination, especially at weekends, when large, straggling groups are likely to be an irritation. Reflect that Wainwright complained about the crowds in 1960!

This shorter (but still substantial and worthwhile) circuit omits the final section over Wetherlam. An interesting climb, much of which is through old mine workings, is followed by an excellent high-level walk along a broad ridge – which made it into Wainwright's "finest ridge-walks" list. The first part of the descent requires some care but otherwise is easy. Unusually, both ascent and descent pass directly by sizeable and attractive mountain tarns.

Summits visited	Coniston Old Man (2633ft/803m) Brim Fell (2611ft/796m) Swirl How (2630ft/ 802m)
Start	Coniston village
Distance	8 miles/12.75km
Height gain	2930ft/890m
Time	6 hours
Map	OS Explorer OL6 (South-western)
Facilities	The main village car park has toilets and an Information Centre which is open daily from 0930 to 1700. There are shops, plenty of accommodation and many places to eat and drink in the village

Parking: Park on the main car park in the centre of Coniston village (SD 303975). On non-school days, there is additional parking in the John Ruskin School on Lake Road; this is reached by leaving the village centre southwards and turning left at the crossroads by the garage. If all else fails there is a sizeable car park at the far end of Lake Road close to the lake, but starting here adds a mile to the round trip.

The walk

Turn left out of the main car park and at the T-junction walk up the lane by the bridge signposted to the Sun Hotel. Immediately beyond the hotel go right (signed Coniston Old Man and Levers Water) and at the end of the short lane continue through the waymarked gate along the track. This passes a building which is part of Coniston's hydro-electric scheme, and climbs gently through a gate/kissing gate above Church Beck to arrive at Miners Bridge. Do not cross this but continue on the path ahead with the stream on your right. Go through a kissing gate adjacent to the business end of the hydro scheme and continue on the well graded path up the valley with its many old spoil heaps and other signs of former mining activity. Soon a broader panorama opens out ahead with Coniston Old Man to the left and the ridge along which we will return to its right.

The path levels and becomes grassier, going through a gap in one wall and a kissing gate in a second before rising to meet the broad stony track coming from the car park at the top of the Walna Scar road. Turn right onto it and in a few yards fork left. The stony path now climbs somewhat roughly up through old mine workings, past ruined buildings and across old cableways, all of which are worthy of pauses for further examination. Approaching the top of the old workings, a point is reached where there is a level on the left with a well preserved entrance, and above it a prostrate cableway tower; here look for a junction and turn right. Soon the climb eases and, as the path runs over a little rise, Low Water appears ahead – a good place for a break.

From here the onward way looks quite uninviting but in fact zig-zags up quite easily helped by some pitching and steps. Soon to the right appears the grassy ridge top going over Brim Fell and Swirl How to Wetherlam, which is seen behind Levers Water. The cairn and massive stone structure on the summit of the Old Man are now only a couple of minutes away. From the summit, the view is extensive, the gems being Morecambe Bay with the estuaries of the Kent, Leven and Duddon to the south, the Scafell group to the north-west, and the magnificent rock wall of Dow Crag between them.

Leave northwards along the broad ridge which can be seen running on to the cairn on Brim Fell and beyond. Keep to the ridge top to avoid dropping down the path to Goat's Hawse; the path itself is stony but wandering along the nearby cropped turf is a joy. Cross the rocky summit of Brim Fell and descend into the depression of Levers Hawse; on the left the water is Seathwaite Tarn and the hill to its right is Grey Friar. Climb past the subsidiary summit and cross the minor depression to the final slope which leads to the top of Swirl How. The prominent cairn, which stands on the edge of the crags falling into Greenburn, is only marginally lower

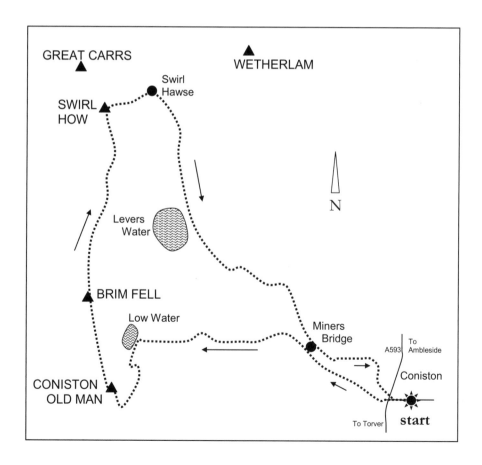

Disused mine workings on the ascent of Coniston Old Man

than that on the Old Man and, being at the northern end of the ridge, is by far the better viewpoint for mountains; the vista round the northern arc from the Scafells to the Helvellyn ridge is particularly good.

Leave the summit eastwards, towards Wetherlam, and start the descent of Prison Band on the well-trodden way. There are a couple of places where hands are needed but taken at a steady pace with pauses to find the easiest way down, there are no difficulties. Soon you arrive at the col of Swirl Hawse, where there is a huge pile of stones.

[From here the circuit could be extended (by 0.75 miles/1km and 500ft/150m of climbing) to include Wetherlam. To do this climb the path ahead and pass the intermediate height of Black Sails on the right to reach its summit. Here turn right and follow the path down Lad Stones ridge to join the Tilberthwaite to Coniston path. Turn right onto this to drop down to join the valley track above Miners Bridge.]

For the main route, turn right at the Hawse onto the very easy path which contours round towards Levers Water. The way becomes indistinct in wet ground a couple of times; at the second, longer and wetter section, keep left along the base of the slope. Pick up the path again as it reappears and follow it down to and along the left-hand side of the water. Pass the dam at the outflow and descend the stony track which heads down towards Coniston, becoming steeper and rougher as it does so. Where the track turns sharply right, go straight on and follow the much better path round the hillside. Continue in the same direction to drop down to the left of the white painted youth hostel and a self-catering block and arrive on their access track. Turn right past the hostel and continue on the track to return past Miners Bridge, again without crossing it. The track shortly becomes metalled and leads into the village.

Walk 13
Seat Sandal

Having set one's sights on the day's summit, it generally seems a good plan to head for it without unnecessary detours or loss of height. Although notes are included to enable those in a tearing hurry to do just that, the main walk here described, which anyway is otherwise rather short, departs from that general principle by including an extension of the route of ascent to include the circumnavigation of one of the area's more famous mountain tarns. The return from the summit, down the mountain's broad, grassy southern ridge, is initially pathless, and in poor visibility requires some navigational skills. Otherwise, it requires only that you pause and consider Wordsworth's assertion that the Vale of Grasmere is "the loveliest spot that man hath ever found".

Summit visited	Seat Sandal (2415ft/736m)
Start	Lay-by on A591, just north of the Swan Hotel, Grasmere
Distance	5.75 miles/9.25km
Height gain	2270ft/690m
Time	5 hours
Map	OS Explorer OL5 (North-eastern) and OL7 (South-eastern)
Facilities	There is a full range of facilities in Grasmere; the toilets are in the Square

Parking: Park in the long lay-by on the northbound side of the A591, just north of the Swan Hotel, Grasmere (NY 337085). Alternatively, it may be preferred to park in the village as this adds only a little to the length of the walk. From the village centre, start off northwards on the B5287, forking left up the narrow lane beyond the Rothay Bridge and then turning left at the main road to quickly reach the lay-by.

The walk

From the lay-by, walk north a short distance on the main road, and, before reaching the Travellers' Rest, find a narrow tarmac drive on the right with a Public Footpath finger post, and signed Winterseeds, Stone Arthur Cottage, Meadow Brow. Go up the drive, following it as it does a dog-leg left, then where it swings left again into Meadow Brow, go straight on, as directed by the finger post, through a metal gate into the parking area of Stone Arthur Cottage. Leave it again almost immediately through a second metal gate, then swinging right, as directed by the waymark, to pass through a gateway. Immediately turn left, then shortly swing left again to quickly leave the field through a gate hidden in the corner. Walk along the track and after 50yds turn right at a waymark post and walk uphill on a sketchy path, guided by two further waymarks, to reach a kissing-gate in the top wall.

Emerging from the kissing-gate, turn left as directed to follow the path which runs round the hillside within a broad green lane. This rises easily as it bends right around the hillside and provides a pleasant high level walk with Helm Crag occupying the view left, and our destination, Seat Sandal, soon appearing directly ahead beyond the gate at the end of the enclosed lane. Continue ahead on a generally level course, as bidden by the waymark, to shortly join the clear path rising from Tongue Gill and follow it up the valley (on the right-hand side of a wall) heading for Grisedale Hause, the best part of 2 miles/3.25km distant. The onward path, which is a part of the Coast to Coast walk, climbs very easily for most of its course, with Seat Sandal high on the left-hand skyline and the ridge leading to the summit of Fairfield ahead. Approaching some crags the mostly paved path steepens as it zig-zags up besides an attractive waterslide. However the gradient soon eases again and the path traverses a level section before it finally climbs to the skyline, beyond which a gap in the broken wall at the Hause is half a minute away. On the right the wall climbs away, accompanied by a rough path, to the summit of Fairfield. Ahead is Grisedale Tarn and behind it Dollywaggon Pike with the repaired path to Helvellyn zig-zagging up its slope.

From here, the summit of Seat Sandal could be reached directly by going half-left for 25yds on a grassy path below the remains of the collapsed wall, and then scaling the steep grass slope beyond it to the summit. However, the recommended walk chooses a slightly circuitous route which takes in a pleasant circumnavigation of Grisedale Tarn. So continue

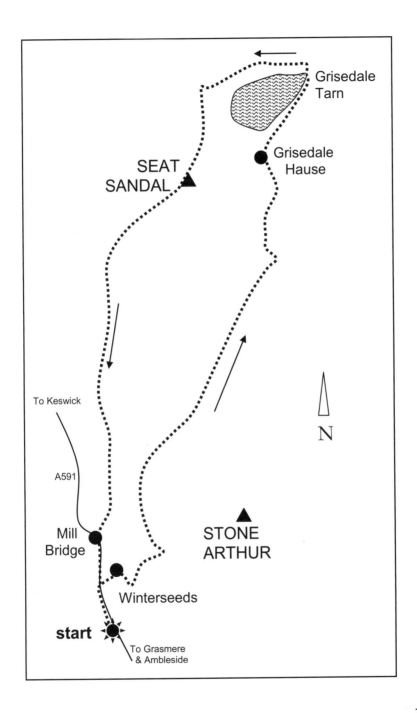

Grisedale
Tarn

Grisedale
Hause

SEAT
SANDAL

To Keswick

A591

N

Mill
Bridge

STONE
ARTHUR

Winterseeds

start

To Grasmere
& Ambleside

on the main path for a stroll down to the outlet of the tarn. As the tarn is approached, there opens up a view down Grisedale to Ullswater, with St Sunday Crag on the right beyond Fairfield. Cross the outlet and keep left round the tarn to join the path which rises up Grisedale and continues up Dollywaggon Pike. Climb on this broad path to its first zig-zag (actually a 90 degrees right turn), and here continue straight on, heading for the top (right-hand) end of a low crag 50yds away. There is no path at first but a faint trod is picked up half way to the outcrop. This trod swings right to join another thin but clearer path. Go left to pass above the outcrop and continue on this fairly level path, which is a bit wet in places, as it runs along above the tarn.

As the slopes of Seat Sandal are approached, ignore the clear path going off left and heading back round the contour towards the Hause from which we came, and keep straight on to a large boulder. Here turn right for 20yds to reach a solitary old fence post. Turn left and follow the path

Grisedale Tarn and St Sunday Crag seen on the final climb to the summit

up the short but steep grassy slope by another broken wall, stepping right over it at the top to reach the summit cairn. The view behind is restricted by the nearby fells, but that to the high, distant mountains in the west is excellent.

To start the grassy descent, which is initially pathless, leave the summit south of west along the ridge and walk to a prominent cairn. Pause to admire the improved view of Thirlmere with Skiddaw behind to the right, and the Vale of Grasmere – village and lake, to the left. Go forward to a second prominent cairn a few yards away, and here bend slightly left, to now travel roughly south-west towards a prominent tarn across the other side of the valley. Here you will find a thin trod, which initially is not easy to see underfoot, but is clearly visible a little way ahead. This developing path continues in the same general direction until, just past a little ruined fenced enclosure, it swings left and heads for Grasmere, down the narrowing ridge, to reach a kissing gate in the intake wall; go through.

Continue down to, and through, the gate in the next cross-wall (ignoring the gate on the left), then moving slightly left to pass through the gap at the end of the next cross-wall (ignoring the gap on the left) and join a broad grassy track. This shortly swings right, and a barn appears half-left. Drop off the track towards the barn and go through the gate to its left. Turn right onto the stony track and follow this down to the main road at Mill Bridge, where turn left to return to the car.

Walk 14
The south-eastern corner

On the very edge of the National Park, passed by visitors arriving from the south even before they first glimpse Lake Windermere, are some mountain-girt valleys which are well worth a visit. The best of these is Kentmere, reached by turning off the main A591 at Staveley, which offers some pleasant and generally quiet walking, although its approach road is narrow and its parking limited. The route described is an easy excursion of moderate length which visits the valleys "own" Pike, and returns pleasantly along the high ground between Kentmere and Longsleddale. The sketchiness of some sections of the ascent path makes it difficult to follow in mist.

Summits visited	**Kentmere Pike (2397ft/730m)** **Shipman Knotts (1926ft/587m)**
Start	**Kentmere Village**
Distance	**6.5 miles/10.5km**
Height gain	**1980ft/604m**
Time	**4.75 hours**
Map	**OS Explorer OL7 (South-eastern)**
Facilities	**There are shops and eating places in Staveley on the main street and in the Mill Yard, where there also is parking**

Parking: Parking in Kentmere Village is limited. Park in the small parking area or the roadside spaces adjacent to the Church and Village Institute (NY 456041). There may also be additional parking in a small field on the left on the approach to the village – just before crossing the river at Low Bridge (NY 458039). There is also space to park 5 or 6 cars on the side of the road beyond the gate on High Lane, at NY 465050; if starting from here, join the walk at the end of the first paragraph.

The head of Kentmere and Ill Bell ridge

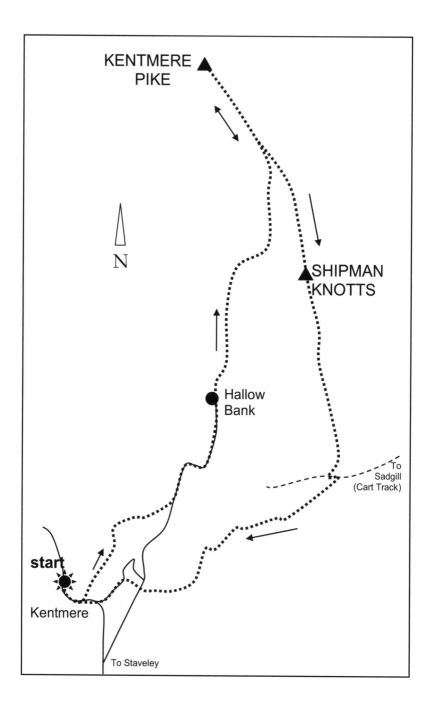

KENTMERE PIKE

SHIPMAN KNOTTS

N

Hallow Bank

start

Kentmere

To Sadgill (Cart Track)

To Staveley

The walk

Start up the narrow lane on the right-hand side of the Church (signed Upper Kentmere and Kentmere Reservoir), and almost immediately take the right fork. Walk along the track to a junction and here bear right to go through a waymarked gate and cross the cobbled area in front of a house. Continue on the now walled track and shortly, where it gradually descends, take a squeeze stile on the right and drop down to the footbridge across the River Kent. Immediately over the bridge, take the left fork and climb up the field to the stile which gives access to Low Lane, a narrow walled bridleway. Go straight across, climb another stile out of the lane and walk up the field to a stile onto a tarmac road (High Lane). Turn left onto the narrow road, going through a gate and passing the parking space mentioned above.

Continue past the stony track to Longsleddale going off right, and the lane to Mardale dropping left, and at the next fork, just before the tarmac road has a "Private Road" sign, go left. Proceed through a gateway into the settlement of Hallow Bank, keeping right of the dwellings to pass through the gate onto the fellside. Bear slightly left to pass to the right of a ruin and gain height easily on a stony path which climbs roughly parallel to, but at some distance from, a wall on the left.

Look for the point at which the path swings left over a little rise and can be seen heading for a gap in this wall, and in a few paces find, and follow, an initially indistinct narrow trod which forks right off the major way and continues to rise with the wall still on the left. A little further up there is a second fork, which may be unclear in wet ground, where the left-hand way runs to a higher gap in the wall; again keep right to reach a third gap in the wall where there is a post with very faded waymarkers. Cross the wall and continue to climb on the indistinct and slightly wet path which heads up to the right of the highest point on the skyline. Pass to the right of a ruin and to the left of an untidy pile of stones. The path becomes drier and heads north towards a ladder stile which appears in a wall three-quarters of the way up to the skyline. The path becomes broad, grassy and almost level, crosses the ladder stile and continues up the hillside to a stone wall, which the path swings left to run beside. As the highest ground is approached, there is a stile in the wall, immediately beyond which is the Ordnance Survey column marking the summit of Kentmere Pike, from where there is an extensive view south to Morecambe Bay.

Leave the summit the way you arrived, but as the ground begins to fall away and the wall on the left becomes a fence, keep left to walk parallel to it down hill. Shortly the fence bends left, but the path goes straight on down a significant groove to a ladder stile. Go over and continue on the clear path, latterly in the company of a wall, to the top of Shipman Knotts.

Continue on down, following the line of the wall. This is an interesting and straightforward descent, despite some stonier sections and some wet patches. Many minor variations from the major route are possible, but as long as the ridge wall is kept in sight, all lead to the same place – the major track crossing from Kentmere to Longsleddale. Turn left onto this track, go through the gate, then turn immediately right and immediately right again through a kissing gate onto the green path which heads off round the flank of the hill. Beyond a gated step stile, the path fades in a grassy area; here keep direction (towards a field gate) and move left to find the path again as it swings left to run parallel to a wall. Over a slight rise the village appears and the path drops down through a number of gates, the last of which has a fingerpost (Longsleddale) and leads onto a gravel lane adjacent to the "Old Forge".

Go left down the lane, which becomes metalled, and turn right at the T-junction. In 20 yards cross a stile on the left and walk down the pasture, trending slightly left to pick up a path which goes over a stile and then down through trees to rejoin the tarmac lane. Turn left, go down to the T-junction and turn right to return to the Church.

Walk 15
Rossett Pike and Angle Tarn

Rossett Pike towers over, and provides an aerial prospect of, the deep cleft of Mickleden, the northern of the two valleys branching from the head of Great Langdale. Yet despite the steep and uninviting prospect it offers to the valley, its ascent (and descent) is easily achieved thanks to the two well-engineered passes which cross its flanks, and the fact that its hidden, western aspect is grassy. On the return a short detour to Angle Tarn is recommended for a warm afternoon. The pleasant walk along Mickleden has to be done on both outward and return legs, but if this is considered a disadvantage, it is more than amply compensated by the proximity of a bar to the car park!

Summit visited	Rossett Pike (2106ft/642m)
Start	Dungeon Ghyll Old Hotel, Great Langdale
Distance	7.75 miles/12.5km
Height gain	1960ft/600m
Time	5.5 hours
Map	OS Explorer OL6 (South-western)
Facilities	Both hotels have bars adjacent to the public car parks where alcoholic drinks, tea, coffee and food are available. There is a large well stocked co-op shop with a café in Chapel Stile. There are toilets on the National Trust car park at the New Hotel

Parking: Park in the National Trust pay and display car park at Dungeon Ghyll Old Hotel (NY 286060), where there is space for 25-30 cars. If this is full, adjacent to the New Hotel (0.5 miles/0.75km nearer Ambleside) there is a National Park Authority pay and display car park across the road from the hotel and a large National Trust pay and display car park next to it. From the lower end of the latter car park, a field path runs along the valley floor the good half mile to the Old Hotel.

The walk

Walk round the back of the Old Hotel on the tarmac access road, continuing on the track running towards the head of the valley, as directed firstly by a 'Path' and then a 'Mickleden' sign. Continue on the easy, pleasant and almost level track, through a number of gates, up Mickleden, with our destination, Rossett Pike directly ahead; the steep slopes on the right rise to Pike o' Stickle, whilst on the left is The Band, a ridge of Bowfell. After nearly 2 miles/3km, nearing the head of the valley, the track reaches a footbridge by a sheepfold. Here turn right on the route shown by guidestones to be the Cumbria Way heading for Stake Pass. Climb this well graded and mostly paved path which zig-zags up the fellside, crosses Stake Beck and then continues on a much more level course to reach the prominent cairn at Stake Pass – the highest point on the crossing to Borrowdale.

Here leave the major route, which drops into Langstrath, and take the path on the left which crosses some wet ground before swinging left and rising up the crest of the ridge leading to Rossett Pike. Approaching the

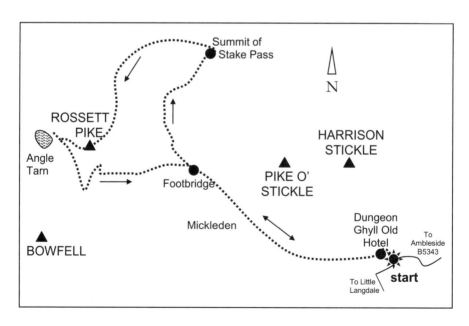

The Langdale Co-op with its unusual "Wanted" sign

col, beyond which the Pike is clearly seen ahead, in front of Bowfell, the main path, which passes to the right of the Pike, begins to drop away slightly to the right on its way to Angle Tarn. So here drift left to find a narrow path which swings left into the col and wander an interesting and easy course amongst the rocks to the left of the crest of the ridge to finally arrive at the summit cairn. However do not linger here but turn left and walk the short distance along the summit ridge to the principal cairn perched spectacularly looking down Mickleden to the head of Great Langdale, with the slopes of Lingmoor Fell beyond. The nearby crags of Bowfell, seen south-westwards across the gash of Rossett Gill, are also a fine sight.

It may be imagined that the way down from this distinct summit might be somewhat precipitous, but in fact it turns out to be an extremely straightforward descent. Start by heading slightly north of west to traverse the short summit ridge; pass the summit cairn and reach rocks nearby which probably just overtop it. Continue in the same direction and you will soon see a narrow but clear path which runs easily and quickly down the simple slope to join the Rossett Gill path at a large cairn near to its highest point. The onward way is to the left, but if it is a warm afternoon and there is time to spare, a detour down to Angle Tarn for a laze on its shore may be tempting. Then commence the return by following the major path over Rossett Pass and on down the repaired, stepped path which does a big zig-zag to the right before returning easily to the footbridge and sheepfold in the valley. From here retrace your steps back down Mickleden to the car. If returning to the New Hotel, remain on the main path which passes above the Old Hotel to continue down the valley.

Walk 16
Far Easedale and Helm Crag

Because of the resemblance of its distinctive summit rocks to the outline of a lion and a lamb, Helm Crag must be one of Lakeland's best known mountains. The summit in fact turns out to be even more interesting when on the spot than when seen from afar and this, combined with its fine views, make it a more than worthwhile destination. This easy walk is a round tour which begins with a perambulation up one of Lakeland's nicest valleys, continues with a high-level traverse along the ridge leading to Helm Crag, and concludes with a descent which has glorious views of the Vale of Grasmere. The first half of the walk uses the popular route over Greenup Edge from Borrowdale to Grasmere which is now also a part of the Coast to Coast walk.

Summits visited	**Calf Crag (1762ft/537m)** **Gibson Knott (1379ft/420m)** **Helm Crag (1329ft/405m)**
Start	**Grasmere**
Distance	**8 miles/12.75km**
Height gain	**2150ft/650m**
Time	**6 hours**
Map	**OS Explorer OL6 (South-western) and OL7 (South-eastern)**
Facilities	**Grasmere has a number of shops, including a co-op grocer and a post office, and many cafés and hotels with bars. The toilets are in the square adjacent to the Methodist Church**

Parking: Park in Grasmere village. Any of the car parks could be used, but Broadgate National Park pay and display car park, on the right of the B5287 just north of the village (NY 338078) is particularly convenient.

The walk

Leave the Broadgate car park along the access road, turn left, and walk towards the village square. Just as you enter the square, turn right, opposite the bookshop, up Easedale Road. Continue up the tarmac road, noting that just past the Quaker Guest House, Glenthorne, you can escape the traffic for a time by using a permissive path which runs alongside the road and emerges again just before Goody Bridge.

Go straight on at the road junction, and, continue on the tarmac lane, past the entrance to Lancrigg, across an unfenced section and between some houses. At a fork go right (signed Far Easedale, Helm Crag) past a "Not for Cars" sign, and up the rough lane which soon becomes paved and goes past a house.

Go through the wide gate, swing left with the path, and at the junction go straight on, signed Far Easedale and Borrowdale. The path continues clearly up the valley; Sourmilk Gill comes into view on the left, with the popular path to Easedale Tarn climbing across the hillside beyond it. There is a short, steeper, rockier section, after which a delightful perambulation alongside Far Easedale Gill leads to the footbridge at

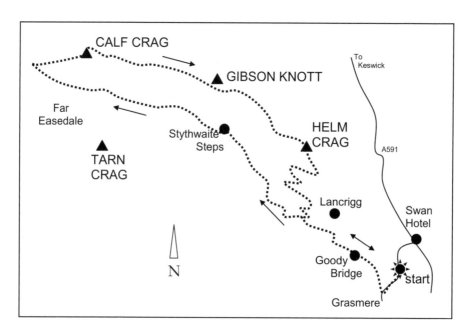

Stythwaite Steps. Cross the bridge, noting on the left the old stepping stones which gave this place its name, and shortly take the right fork to follow the stream up the valley of Far Easedale on a now narrower track. Today's first mountain, Calf Crag, is now directly ahead and the ridge on which we will return is on the right. The path climbs gently and interestingly past some fine crags and waterfalls for a little over 1.5 miles/2.5km to the col at the head the valley, where there is a cairn and a line of old metal fence posts.

Ahead is a hollow, beyond which, almost a mile away and 350ft/110m higher, is Greenup Edge over which the path to Borrowdale can be seen climbing. Other paths follow the fence posts right to Wythburn and left to Sergeant Man. Take none of these. Instead follow the almost level path which doubles back sharp right; the return ridge soon appears and the path leads very quickly and with virtually no further effort to the summit of Calf Crag.

Leave the top just north of east on the initially indistinct path which drops down to follow the ridge along to Helm Crag. The path avoids the crinkly ridge crest, preferring a simpler route along its right hand flank, and passes to the right of the intermediate summit of Gibson Knott, to which the short detour left to its cairn should be made. Continue eastwards on the exquisite narrow path which winds in and out and up and down to reach the depression at the foot of the final slope up to the top of Helm Crag. The final section is a short but steepish climb up a winding rocky way.

The top of Helm Crag is an unusual and interesting place which, despite its modest altitude, made it into Wainwright's top six summits. It takes the form of a lengthy ridge with a striking rock formation at either end, that at the north-west (Gibson Knott) end being popularly known as The Lion and the Lamb. The main cairn lies a little way beyond it.

Leave the summit by continuing on the path south-eastwards in the direction of Grasmere village and lake. The path heads towards a rock tower but drops right before reaching it, and runs on towards the ridge end. However, just before getting there, it swings round right in a wide arc, briefly heading back towards the head of the valley, before resuming its line in the general direction of the village. Continue down on the well-used path which is generally straightforward, although a steep old-pitched section could require care when wet.

The summit ridge of Helm Crag

Towards the valley bottom, at a large cairn, go left down the lane between high walls to return to the three-way finger post which we passed on our outward journey. Go left (signed Grasmere) and then quickly swing right through a wide gate.

However, rather than simply retracing steps to the village, vary your return by taking the short and pleasant detour through the grounds of Lancrigg. To do this, go left immediately after the wide gate through a small gate on the left past a sign which advertises the hotel's restaurant and confirms that this is a permissive path to Grasmere. Then follow the main woodland path or variants on either side of it as shown on an information Board and indicated by plentiful finger-posts. Emerge into a small garden and thence walk across the grass in front of the hotel, climb a few steps and continue down the hotel access drive, keeping straight on at a crosstracks to emerge on the top section of Easedale Road. Head back down the road to the village.

If you need a café, shop or toilet, the recommended return is to follow the roadside footway round to the right of Glenthorne, then keeping left across the grass and turning left on reaching the tarmac road to walk over the cattle grid and into the village. Alternatively, if you are returning directly to the car on Broadgate car park, continue a little further along Easedale Road, going through a gate on the left immediately beyond Silver Lea and walking over Butharlyp Howe. On reaching the main road the car park is a couple of minutes to the right.

Walk 17
Easedale Tarn and Silver How

Although following some popular routes which can be busy, this walk is too good to miss. Its outward leg uses the easy path which climbs by the falls of Sourmilk Gill and then runs alongside Easedale Tarn before climbing onto the ridge linking Blea Rigg and Silver How, along which the return is made. The views of Great Langdale and its encircling mountains are excellent. Either or both of the summits visited on the main walk may be omitted if time or energy is desperately short.

Summits visited	Blea Rigg (1776ft/541m) Silver How (1295ft/395m)
Start	Grasmere village
Distance	7 miles/11.25km
Height gain	2050ft/625m
Time	5 hours
Map	OS Explorer OL7 (South-eastern)
Facilities	Grasmere has shops, accommodation and a good selection of cafés. There are toilets in the Square

Parking: Park in Grasmere village. Any of the car parks could be used, but Broadgate National Park pay and display car park, on the right of the B5287 just north of the village (NY 338078) is particularly convenient.

The walk
If you need to visit the facilities in the village, leave the car park the way you drove in and turn left at the road, taking the first road on the right (Easedale Road), as you enter the Square. Continue on the tarmac, noting

that just past Glenthorne Guest House, you can escape onto a permissive path which runs alongside the road. Alternatively, leave the car park in the corner furthest away from the entrance and walk round two sides of the recreational area (the first being along the riverside), cross the road, turn right for a short distance and then go left through a gate and follow the track over Butharlyp Howe. Turn right at Easedale Road and in a short distance reach the permissive path on the left.

At the end of the permissive path rejoin the tarmac and go straight on at the junction. Where the road swings right, cross the footbridge on the left (signed Easedale Tarn), go through the gate and follow the broad stony track with Easedale Beck on the right. Ahead can be seen the waterfalls of Sourmilk Gill with our path climbing across the hillside above them; the mountain behind is Tarn Crag. Ignore the stone arched bridge on the right and continue on the clear track through a second gate. Take the left-hand fork and follow this through a non-sheep-proof gate to a kissing gate. Only now, some 1.5 miles/2.5km into the walk, does the proper climbing begin. The stony, partly repaired path rises steadily, climbing for a time close to the waterfalls of Sourmilk Gill, and then swinging left to enter a shallow grassy hollow where first-time visitors will, wrongly, expect to find the tarn. So, continue across the hollow and up to the edge beyond – over which the tarn really is!

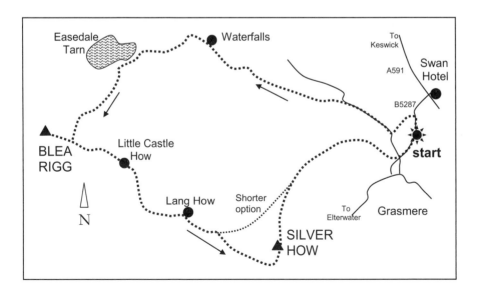

Looking up Easedale to the Sourmilk Gill waterfalls

Shortly then arrive at Easedale Tarn, where a rest on one of the grassy mounds beside the path is in order. Having admired the prospect of the water nestled beneath the steep south-eastern face of Tarn Crag, continue on the same path, with the tarn on the right. Shortly cross a stream and just a little further on arrive at a clear fork marked with a small cairn. Here go left on a grassy path which goes round the left-hand side of a small hillock to climb pleasantly across the hillside. Where the path becomes indistinct, continue along the contour to find it again as it climbs a short stony gulley, at the top of which it swings left to climb, now more steeply but very pleasantly, guided by occasional cairns, towards the skyline. Where the ground levels the path again becomes indistinct, but continue ahead to quickly reach the clear ridge path at a pile of stones.

For a ten minute walk to the summit of Blea Rigg (recommended) turn right onto the ridge path; to miss this out, turn left onto the ridge path and skip the next two paragraphs.

The path to the top climbs a little, crosses some easily angled rock slabs and runs on with high ground up on the right. Eventually the path swings right and appears, at last, to be going to the top, but actually passes to the right of the highest point, before swinging left beyond it to continue along the ridge. So, leave the path on the left and wander up to the highest point, which is a rock on which is balanced a few small stones. Most striking in the view are the lakes of Windermere and Elterwater south-eastwards, and close by westwards, the mountains of Pavey Ark and Harrison Stickle – which will be more attractively seen as we walk along the ridge to Silver How.

Eastwards from here, across the path on which we approached, and just beyond two small tarns, is another rocky high point which appears to be not quite as lofty, although opinions on this differ. You might like to visit it and perhaps amend your view as to which overtops the other; either way there can only be inches in it. Retrace your steps from the summit area and return to the point of arrival on the ridge, here continuing ahead on the clear path.

Note that the top of Silver How is 2 miles/3.25km distant at the extreme far end of the ridge and that on the way to it we will pass a number of intermediate high points.

The way winds interestingly along the broad ridge. Early in the journey there is a grassy downhill section where the path fades completely and then reappears very clearly. Just beyond this the path swings left and joins another path (presumably worn by people coming the other way), onto which turn right. Then, in a few paces, the path goes slightly right and climbs the short, well cairned way up the steepish and rocky intermediate summit of Little Castle How; do not take the tempting thin but clear grass trod which drops gently to the left-hand side of the higher ground.

Beyond the little summit, the path drops steadily into the broad, grassy depression between Blea Rig and Silver How. Just before reaching the bottom of the depression, detour to the right along a short, grassy spur for a superb panorama of the head of Great Langdale. Continue into the depression, leaving it on the main path which fades as it circles round the hillock, to find the clear onward way continuing uphill. On the right the grand views up Great Langdale continue. The path climbs to another hillock, this one with a cairn on top, and contours round its right-hand side, but it would be a shame not to go straight on over it and pick up the path on the other side. Beyond, ignore a thin path going off right, and drop into a small dip with high ground (Lang How) ahead. Here the path turns 90 degrees right, and contours round between the high ground on the left and a big wet depression on the right, before dropping down to pass a reedy tarn. The main path continues ahead and forms a short-cut back to Grasmere, but prefer instead to take either of the two thin grassy paths which set off to the right just beyond the tarn, and follow the winding way to the top of Silver How. The bird's eye view over Grasmere and Rydal is very good.

For the return to the village, pick up the path running northwards. This starts off quite steeply down a short rocky section before ambling on easily on grass to arrive at a slightly awkward rocky descent to the crossing of Wray Gill. On the other side it rises to join the short-cut path which has come directly from the junction by the reedy tarn. Continue down, initially through junipers, then with Grasmere village below, to a kissing gate at the top of a walled lane. Go through and follow the path down, continuing through a kissing gate to reach a tarmac lane. Turn right and follow this back to the Village Square. Turn left for Broadgate car park.

Walk 18
The Fairfield Horseshoe

This is the longest walk in the book and breaks the rule of seeking a route into the hills other than the "tourist" path. It is included because it is a grand high-level walk which is too good to be left out of any walking itinerary based on the Ambleside/Grasmere axis. The route described starts at Rydal and tackles the horseshoe anticlockwise, which gives the easiest walking, and gets the less-interesting flat bit out of the way at the beginning. It also uses a seemingly little-known path which completely avoids the road walking, as well as shaving a mile off the overall distance.

Route finding is generally simple, the way being along the spine of well-defined ridges. However the summit of Fairfield itself can be confusing, and in poor visibility, care is needed to locate the return route.

Summits visited	Low Pike (1667ft/508m) High Pike (2155ft/657m) Dove Crag (2598ft/792m) Hart Crag (2698ft/822m) Fairfield (2863ft/873m) Great Rigg (2513ft/766m) Heron Pike (2008ft/612m) Nab Scar (1450ft/442m)
Start	Rydal Church
Distance	10.25 miles/16.5km
Height gain	3440ft/1050m
Time	6.5 hours
Map	OS Explorer OL5 (North-eastern) and OL7 (South-eastern)
Facilities	The walk starts through the grounds of Rydal Hall, wherein is to be found a tea shop

Facilities (cont'd)	which is open daily from 10am. Adjacent to the Hall itself is a small, formal garden which has recently been restored to much of its former glory and is well worth a visit another day

Parking: In Rydal village, adjacent to the church, turn off the A591 into the private road which runs north and provides access to Rydal Hall and Rydal Mount. Park on the roadside alongside or above the church (NY 364062).

The walk

Walk up the minor road and turn right into the grounds of Rydal Hall at the green signs for the tea shop and gardens, and the finger-post pointing to Ambleside. Follow the access road, which has yellow waymarkers, behind the Hall, past the tea shop and garden entrance, and over the bridge to a junction where you turn left (signed Ambleside). Shortly the track leaves the grounds of the Hall at a gate/stile and continues between fences across parkland. After 0.5 mile/0.75km, look on the left for a wall which comes down the hillside and ends at a short section of fence, and beyond which is a stream (Scandale Beck). You want to turn left off the track to go up the hill on a path between the wall and the stream. To do this, leave the track through a metal gate (partially obstructed by an old metal support), and walk the short distance by the fence to the end of the wall. Here go left on the path which sets off between the wall and the stream, and climb through a few trees to a gate. Go through, and bear right, now with a wall on the right, to shortly arrive at a broad gravel track; turn sharp left uphill on it.

The track winds up through a gate, and then goes through a gap into an area with a few trees. Here keep on the main track, to soon go through another gap in a wall, and arrive at a fork. Either way would take you to Low Pike, but the left-hand route, which runs close to the ridge-top wall, requires the negotiation of a tricky rock step. Therefore take the right-hand way, and keep right again at a second fork to remain on the old cart-track. At a broken wall there is a further fork where either way may be taken to the top of a low rise. From here continue through the gap in the cross-wall ahead, and 40yds further on, where a path goes down right to High Sweden Bridge, keep straight on. The way winds past the end of

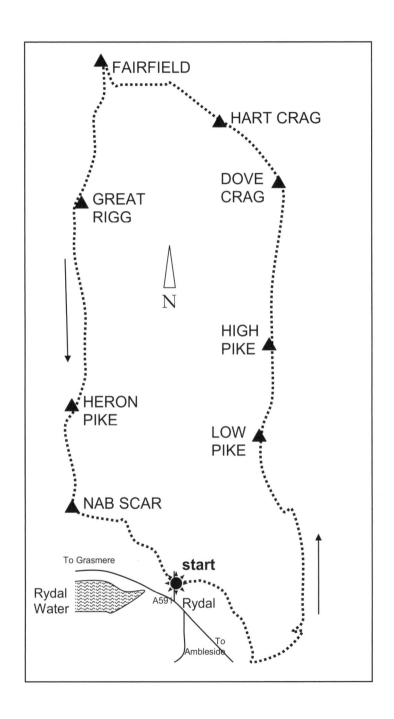

FAIRFIELD

HART CRAG

DOVE
CRAG

GREAT
RIGG

N

HIGH
PIKE

HERON
PIKE

LOW
PIKE

NAB SCAR

To Grasmere

start

Rydal
Water

A591 Rydal

To
Ambleside

Sweden Crag, before climbing left to join the other path and quickly arrive at a step stile over the ridge-top wall.

Cross the stile and continue to climb with the wall on your right. The way along the ridge towards Low Pike, the day's first summit, is now clear. At Low Pike, High Pike comes into view; it looks horribly distant, and indeed is reached only after a stiffish climb. However, here the gradient eases and the way on to Dove Crag is much easier.

At the foot of the final slope to Dove Crag, with its summit cairn clearly visible, cross to the right-hand side of the now broken wall in to order to visit the highest point and admire the extensive view. From here, continue on the clear path by the broken wall, firstly over the summit of Hart Crag, and then on across the depression to finally climb the stony slope onto Fairfield's surprisingly grassy summit plateau, where the broad, cairned path swings right to arrive at the extensive pile of stones-cum-shelter marking the highest point.

The final climb onto Fairfield

From here the view is packed with hills in virtually every direction, the Helvellyn and High Street ridges both being seen particularly well. A visit to the northern cairn for the view of St Sunday Crag beyond Fairfield's much craggier face is worthwhile.

From the summit cairn head off south, which is not far to the right of the arrival path, towards what looks like an untidy pile of stones (and turns out to be a sort of low shelter). Pick up the path which forms almost immediately to begin the long but easy return to Rydal. Having traversed Great Rigg, watch out for the only point where there is a possibility of going wrong. Not far below its summit, where a path runs off right along the branching ridge to Stone Arthur, keep left to follow the clear path along the main ridge top over Heron Pike and on to Nab Scar. Here the gentle gradients we have enjoyed thus far on our descent come to an end, to be replaced for the last thousand feet by much steeper ground. Fortunately the majority of the way down has been constructed and easy stone steps facilitate the return of tired limbs to the valley, the path leading exactly to the top of the lane on which the car is parked.

Walk 19
Aira Force and
the Ullswater balcony path

A short and easy walk visiting the popular Aira Force waterfall and continuing to the summit of nearby Gowbarrow Fell. The return is via a "balcony" path which gives fine views over Ullswater.

Summit visited	Gowbarrow Fell (1579ft/481m)
Start	Aira Force car park
Distance	4 miles/6.75km
Height gain	1080ft/330m
Time	3.25 hours plus time to explore the waterfalls
Map	OS Explorer OL5 (North-eastern)
Facilities	There are toilets in the car park and a tea shop two minutes walk from it

Parking: Park in the National Trust pay and display car park at Aira Force, near the junction of the A592 and A5091, on the northern shore of Ullswater (NY 401201).

The walk

The first priority is an exploration of Aira Force. So, leave the top of the car park through the gate and follow everybody else along the path to the falls. Approaching the stream, you can either keep right to cross a wooden footbridge and take a path up the right-hand (eastern) bank, or go left and take the path climbing on the left-hand (western) bank. Both paths climb past two stone arched bridges over Aira Beck, one immediately below and the other immediately above the main falls, and then continue upstream. If using the left-hand path, you arrive at and cross a final wooden footbridge and continue upstream on the right-hand path. If using the right-hand path above the main falls, note that this by-passes the top wooden bridge, so you will need to detour left down a stony way if you wish to visit it; otherwise continue upstream. In short, it matters not which route you take to explore the falls, as long as you conclude your visit by heading upstream from the top wooden bridge on the right-hand side of the stream.

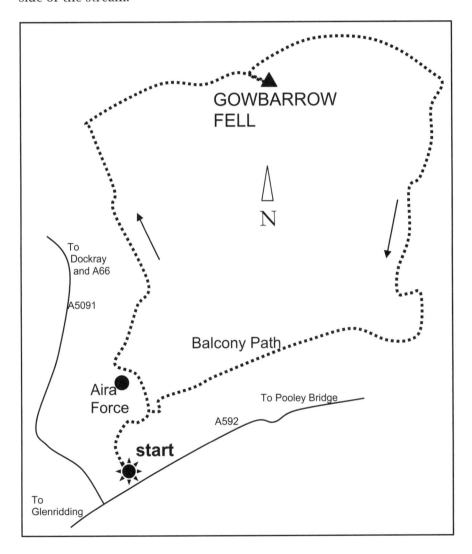

Continue on the clear path, which runs close to the stream at a delightful spot where the water flows over stone slabs, and pass through a gap in a wall to leave the woodland through a gate in a fence. Approaching the next gate in a wall, do not go through it but follow a grassy path which branches off right and climbs to a ladder stile by a gate. Cross the stile and continue climbing up the repaired, partially stepped path beside the wall where a nice view of the head of Ullswater opens up on the right. The wall bends left and the path follows it. On the steeper section, the path drifts away from the wall to the right but returns to it as the gradient eases and the triangulation column on the top of Gowbarrow Fell comes into view half-right. Continue by the wall on what can be a rather wet section until, approaching where the wall reaches its highest point, the main path swings right to cross to the triangulation column, with National Trust plaque affixed, on the summit. The panorama would not win prizes, as much of it, including most of the lake, is obscured by the edges of the fell's broad summit. However, the views on the return to the valley more than make up for this.

Ullswater and Sheffield Pike from the slopes of Gowbarrow Fell

Leave the top north-eastwards (from the side of the column opposite that with the plaque) on a clear path which drops down a bit rockily. If the stones are wet and muddy, this initial section can be a bit awkward, and it is then easier to leave the top by the arrival path and at the bottom of the short initial steeper section, to turn right on a clear, thin path which drops gently to join the direct path.

Beyond this junction, the descending path can be very muddy after rain, and diversions to the right may be helpful to avoid the worst of the slipperiness. A wall comes in from the left (it is the wall we followed on our ascent) and as we approach it, our path swings right and continues its gentle descent parallel to it, keeping the wall on the left, down a shallow valley towards Ullswater.

Shortly the mud ends and the path arrives at a ruin on the left, marked as a Shooting Lodge on the OS map, and just beyond this, at a Y-junction, where we keep right on a clear path running west of south. This path initially does a short sharp climb but then levels and begins to fall gently as it winds its way round the hillside. Initially there is a short section where the ground falls away steeply on the left but the exposure is not great.

At Yew Crag the view of the lake opens out southwards so virtually the whole of its length is seen. There is a cairn on a promontory, accessed by a step-stile in a fence, from which the views both along and across the lake are glorious. A few paces further on, to the right of the path, there is a stone bench, on the back of which is the inscription "A thank-offering October 1905".

The easy path continues on, high above the lake, on a good, wide shelf before finally beginning to loose height as it drops easily down a stony, partly stepped section. It then levels and moves away from the lake, to approach the Aira Force site. Keep left at a fork to enter the site through a gate, left again to walk down by a wooden fence, and left again to cross the wooden footbridge and return to the car park.

Walk 20
Mardale Head

There are two Harter Fells in the Lake District, one towards its western edge at the head of Eskdale, and the other near its eastern extremity at the head of Mardale. This walk climbs the latter of these which stands at the head of Haweswater and dominates the view up the valley on the approach alongside the reservoir. Wainwright describes the circuit to the summit from Mardale Head as "an excellent expedition, richly rewarding in intimate scenes of Harter Fell's grand northern cliffs and in the views of Haweswater from its summit, yet short in distance and needing much less effort in execution than its formidable appearance suggests." He is, as always, absolutely right. The outward and return routes from the valley use the old routes to Kentmere and to Longsleddale from what was the hamlet of Mardale Head, prior to its drowning in the reservoir.

Summit visited	Harter Fell (2552ft/778m)
Start	Mardale Head
Distance	4.25 miles/6.75km
Height gain	1750ft/530m
Time	3.5 hours
Map	OS Explorer OL5 (North-eastern)
Facilities	None. There is a shop with a tea room, and a pub in Bampton

Parking: Park at the head of Haweswater (NY 469107) where there is room for a total of around two dozen cars in a car park and spaces marked on the adjacent road. If all this is full, there are a couple of small roadside spaces nearby, but there is a consensus that the road hereabouts, constructed when the valley was flooded, is wide enough for parking on the road itself.

The walk

Leave the parking area at the road end through the kissing gate by the old but well maintained MCWW (Manchester Corporation Water Works) signpost. The sign also claims to be a bus stop, although a nearby notice points out that the nearest real bus stop is in Burnbanks, 5 miles/8km back up the valley.

Through the gate, almost immediately a junction with a short finger-post and a choice of three onward ways is reached; take the middle way, signed Nan Bield Pass and Kentmere. Follow the clear, easy path through a gate next to a nailed-up kissing gate, up a broad valley with many moraines, and through the gate in the intake wall. Climbing the valley, our objective is up on our left, and Mardale Ill Bell lies ahead, with High Street to its right; behind, the view down Haweswater gradually opens up. Above the gate, the path continues easily, moving closer to the delightful Small

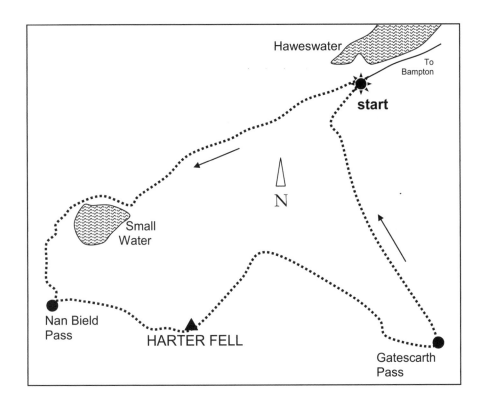

Water Beck, and climbing to reach the outflow from Small Water, which nestles in a coomb between Harter Fell and Mardale Ill Bell. The path crosses the outflow from the tarn and continues round the right-hand side of the water.

Alongside the path, overlooking Small Water, are three small, low, square, roofed shelters which have been built with some care and skill – probably some time ago, and which remain in amazingly good condition. They are unlike any others found in the district and presumably were built as shelter for travellers of some sort using this old route between Mardale and Kentmere, although why here and not on any of the other old tracks in the district is unknown. Beyond the tarn, the path begins its climb up the slope to Nan Bield Pass, which is accomplished much more easily than early views of the way ahead from besides the tarn suggested. Arriving at the Pass, which has a good shelter with a substantial stone seat, Kentmere lies ahead with Ill Bell, which assumes its more familiar shape during the onward climb, rising above the reservoir.

Leave the shelter to the left and embark on the straightforward climb to the summit of Harter Fell. Approaching the cairn on the edge of the summit plateau, either go straight up a rocky section with the main path, or take a smaller path which does a detour left around the rocky bit.

From the cairn, the path runs forward to two further cairns, the second of which, which stands just before a fence is reached, marks the highest point. The view from here is extensive and takes in Morecambe Bay to the south, the Howgill Fells and Pennines to the east, and the Coniston, Scafell and Helvellyn ranges to the west. Surprisingly, the fell's namesake, 16 miles/28km away at the head of Eskdale, also makes an appearance.

Do not cross the fence, but leave the summit left and walk along the grassy promenade, with the fence on your right, towards cairns at the far side of the summit plateau. On arrival it will be found that there are two significant but untidy piles of stones, one of which sprouts bits of old metal fence posts. From here the view is not much changed except for the appearance of Blea Water beneath the crags between Mardale Ill Bell and High Street.

Commence the descent by continuing in the same direction, still with the fence on the right, to where it does a sharp right turn. Here step left a few

Leaving the shelter on Nan Bield Pass

paces for a striking aerial view of Haweswater and the car park, before continuing the easy descent, still with the fence on the right but now on a constructed path. Further down the slope the fence detours to the right but the path prefers a more direct route down to Gatesgarth Pass where we turn left onto the clear track coming over from Longsleddale. An easy descent on the broad, well-graded track takes us back down to the valley, where after crossing the intake wall using a ladder stile next to a locked gate, we quickly arrive back at the three way junction adjacent to the parking area.

Walk 21
Angletarn Pikes

The double summit of Angletarn Pikes is a distinctive landmark in views around the Patterdale valley, and makes the hill readily identifiable even when seen from afar. Although not particularly lofty, the Pikes make an enjoyable climb, and their summits, particularly the higher northern one, are delectable places to be – easily attainable, yet forming splendid grassy perches which feel every inch real mountain tops. From here are seen panoramas in which Helvellyn and its illustrious neighbours crowd the skyline, and the Vale of Patterdale makes a delightful foreground. This straightforward circular walk takes in both of the mountain's summits as well as including a visit to the Pikes very own mountain tarn, and a gentle exploration of the neighbouring valley and fell.

Summits visited	Angletarn Pike North (1857ft/567m) Angletarn Pike South (1854ft/565m)
Start	Hartsop village
Distance	6.5 miles/10.5km
Height gain	1640ft/500m
Time	4.25 hours
Map	OS Explorer OL5 (North-eastern)
Facilities	In Patterdale there are toilets, a shop/post office, an inn and a hotel

Parking: Travelling south from Patterdale on the A592, after nearly 2 miles/3km, a minor road on the left gives access to Hartsop village. Drive along this through the village to the parking area at the very end of the road (NY 410131). If this is full, return to the main road and go right 400yds to Cow Bridge car park (see Walk 23). To start the walk from here, return towards Hartsop village, but just after turning off the main road, turn left again along a minor road which continues as an unsurfaced bridleway heading for Patterdale. After 0.5 miles/1km, just after the footbridge over Angletarn Beck, start reading at the beginning of the second paragraph. At the end of the walk continue down the tarmac lane through the village.

The walk

Leave the car park the way you drove in (back towards the village) and shortly go right, at the footpath sign, through the gate and up a concreted track. Pass through a second gate and over the rise, continuing straight on, as directed by the waymarks, to arrive at the garden fence of Grey Rigg Cottage. Turn right along a narrower path, go through the gate and follow the rough, wet path which gradually loses height to run along above the intake wall, where it becomes grassier. Go through the gate in the cross-wall, ford the stream and drop down to join the bridleway coming from the left.

Continue on the bridleway to a major junction of tracks (just before a warning notice to cyclists), and here fork right to climb on the pleasant well-graded track which rises to Boredale Hause.

Shortly before arriving at the Hause, a clear path from Patterdale joins from the left, and just beyond this junction is a cairn. Advance to the cairn, leaving it again on the path half-right, to cross the beck and climb up the path beyond. Pass a huge (and pointless) cairn and continue on the well-used path to a fork. Here go left, heading for the northernmost of the two Angletarn Pikes, which is now directly above.

Then, just before passing in front of the Pike, turn left off the path to follow a clear thin trod, which sets off in the depression between the Pike on the right and a minor hump on the left. Follow this trod past the Pike, keeping right at a fork and swinging right again as it rises to run along the right-hand side of the summit ridge to the diminutive cairn at its south-west end. Here sit on the cropped grass of this splendid little summit and unhurriedly enjoy the prospect of the lovely panorama of Fairfield and the Helvellyn ridge with the jewel of Brothers Water set in the valley below.

There are many routes to our next port of call – the other (southern) Pike; the suggestion is to set off south-westwards on the clear path which descends towards Brothers Water, noting as you go a good route across the marshy depression and up the grassy slope beyond. On arrival, the view is found to be much as before but with the notable addition of Angle Tarn with our onward path running round its shore towards High Street.

There is no obvious path down to the tarn but a trod which leaves the cairn south-westwards and quickly doubles back and winds downwards

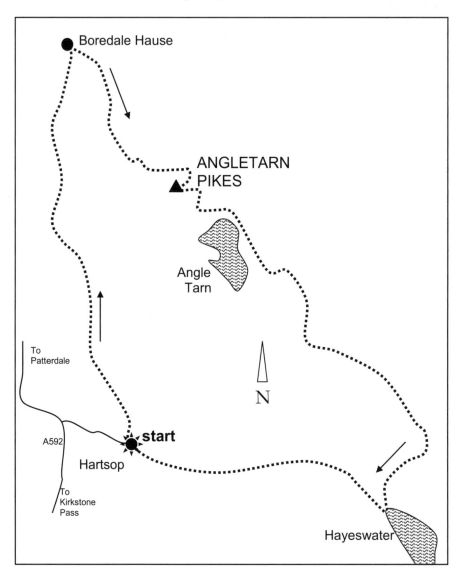

Angle Tarn

is a good start. Then pick a way between rocky outcrops using various sheep tracks and trods to re-join the main path, turning left on it to reach the tarn. Having paused at the water's edge to enjoy the attractive interplay of land and water, continue on the well-worn way. Shortly, keep a look out for a single old fence post to the left, and here climb up off the path for a few paces onto the grassy top of the ridge for a good view of Bannerdale beyond. Then, to keep the open outlook to the left for a few minutes more, follow the trod along the grassy ridge top and then along a line of old fence posts to a high point, where it is necessary to drop down half-right back onto the main path to cross a wall at a gateway.

Beyond, the rough path climbs gradually above the mostly broken wall, detouring round many puddles. Approaching the top of the rise, leave the clearer way which goes off half-left towards Rest Dodd, and take the narrower path which continues parallel to the wall, which soon becomes a fence. Go right with the fence at the corner and follow it as it reverts to being a wall. Shortly the wall drops away right slightly whilst the path continues on the contour, drops to cross a stream and then climbs a short distance towards a cross-wall with gaps. Just before the wall, branch off right (to cut off a corner), go through the wall and turn right down grass to shortly join a wider path coming down from the left. Follow this down easy grass and across the footbridge by the dam at the outflow of Hayeswater. Go up to the stony track and turn right to follow this via two gates, one bridge and a cattle grid back to the car park.

Walk 22
Sheffield Pike

Sheffield Pike is not one of Lakeland's best known hills, but its ascent from Glenridding is as pleasant and as varied a medium length mountain walk as any in the district. The route described makes the short detour to the top of Glenridding Dodd, for an aerial view of the village and the foot of the Ullswater, before tackling the climb up the mountain's interesting south-east ridge. The return is via the Glencoyne valley and Ullswater's lakeshore.

Summits visited	Glenridding Dodd (1450ft/442m) Sheffield Pike (2215ft/675m)
Start	Glenridding
Distance	5.5 miles/8.75km
Height gain	1920ft/590m
Time	4.5 hours
Map	OS Explorer OL5 (North-eastern)
Facilities	The car park has toilets and an Information Centre which is open daily from 0930 to 1730. The village has shops, and a choice of eating places and accommodation

Parking: Park on the large National Park pay and display car park in the centre of Glenridding (NY 385170).

The walk
With the Information Centre behind you walk up the little tarmac path just to the left of Fellbites café. Slant right across the car park exit road, in front of Fairlight café, and cross the minor motor road (Greenside Road) to a finger post indicating a path to Greenside. Follow this through a gate and round a play area to a kissing gate. Go through and follow the

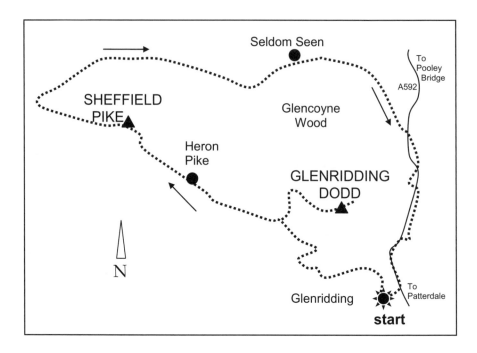

waymarked path which rises up the field and then swings left parallel to a wall to arrive at a narrow metal kissing gate where large rucksacks will need to be removed. Continue up the grassy track through a gate and turn left onto a vehicle track. Go through a metal gate to quickly arrive back at Greenside Road opposite a letter box, and turn right uphill (signed Greenside Mine and Sticks Pass).

Pass some houses on the right and continue to a cattle grid with a sign "Glenridding Common". Cross this and immediately fork right off the rough road onto a grassy track which climbs towards a higher terrace of houses. About two-thirds of the way to the houses, climb a narrow path up the grass bank on the right to very quickly arrive at another grass track with a waymarker indicating a narrow stony path which climbs the steep hillside.

Here commence the ascent proper. The way is initially rough but quickly improves. By a rocky knoll go left to continue climbing (after detouring a short distance ahead for the view), and soon arrive at the col between Glenridding Dodd on the right and Sheffield Pike on the left. A wall crosses this col and the path we are on goes to a gate in it. However, we fork right just before reaching it to take a short cut across the corner and continue up a stony path with a wall on the left. Then, where the wall starts to descend, turn sharp right and continue to climb around the fellside. The path soon levels and arrives at the summit cairn on Glenridding Dodd. However, don't stop here, but continue on the path towards the lake and fork right, to reach a grander and altogether more impressive cairn perched on the edge overlooking the village, or fork left to a slightly more distant and lower cairn looking up the length of Ullswater.

Return to the summit and retrace your steps to the col, approaching which keep right to follow the wall down. Cross the path to the gate, and take the left fork. Our path now crosses a broken wall and then winds its way interestingly, and generally clearly, up the ridge, to arrive, in due course at a level section. Here a path goes off right to the nearby Heron Pike, on which are a small cairn commanding a view of the lake and mountains beyond which is probably better than that from the summit, and an old metal boundary post marked H on one side and M on the other,

The village and lake from Glenridding Dodd

and dated 1912. (At least one other similar post lies near the path used for the descent.) Return to the main path, traverse the level section and ascend the short steeper climb to the summit plateau, continuing on the faint path to the cairn and shelter on the top of Sheffield Pike.

Leave the summit on the path running westwards, in the direction of the old spoil heaps, and descend towards the col between Sheffield Pike and Stybarrow Dodd. Approaching the lowest point, keep right and pick up the path running down the valley of Glencoyne. The path drops easily down to a gate in the intake wall. Go through and continue down, mostly on grass, with a wall on the left, to a wall corner. Continue ahead over a stile and down through trees still with the wall on the left. Pass behind the row of houses at the aptly named Seldom Seen, and arrive on their access track. Continue on this for approaching half a mile to where, just beyond some huge boulders in front of an extraordinarily mossy wall on the left, the track does a distinct left turn. Here take the clear thin path which goes off half-right and, sadly at this late stage in the walk, climbs a short distance over a rise in the woodland. Continue down the other side, passing through a gate, to reach the main road at a finger-post. Cross the road carefully and turn right to join the path which runs beside, but off, the tarmac. After 50yds the path drops left to continue a little further away from the road until a stream running down into the lake bars further progress and the path ends.

Those with a burning desire to stand with their toes in the lake, can easily do so from here by detouring the short distance over grass to the gravelly lakeshore. Otherwise go up to the road for a short section of road walking which cannot be completely avoided, although some relief may be gained by crossing over to the metal gates of Hawkhow, and continuing on the grass verge and then through the wide lay-by. Unfortunately for 70yds beyond it, where the road swings right round Stybarrow Crag, there is briefly no escape at all from the carriageway, so great care is necessary. Then, as soon as the road starts to move away from the water, take the path on the left which continues very pleasantly close to the lakeside.

Go up the steps past two seats and continue on the path by the water's edge. After passing another seat, the path swings away from the water and zig-zags up some steps to emerge back on the main road by the "Glenridding" sign. Turn left along the pavement to quickly reach the village centre and car park.

Walk 23
High level Dovedale

This is a straightforward high level walk around the rim of Dovedale. The route described visits five summits and takes in some excellent mountain scenery. The highest section of the walk, from Hart Crag to Dove Crag, is a part of the Fairfield Horseshoe

Summits visited	Hartsop above How (1870ft/570m) Hart Crag (2698ft (822m) Dove Crag (2598ft/792m) Little Hart Crag (2091ft/637m) High Hartsop Dodd (1702ft/519m)
Start	Cow Bridge
Distance	7.25 miles/11.75km
Height gain	2710ft/830m
Time	5.75 hours
Map	OS Explorer OL5 (North-eastern)
Facilities	There are a shop, a pub and a hotel, and toilets in Patterdale

Parking: Park in the National Park Authority car park at Cow Bridge (NY 403134), just over 1.5 miles/2.75km south of Patterdale on the west side of the A592, and just north of the end of the minor road into Hartsop village. The car park has two sections, one on each side of Goldrill Beck. Each section has its own access from the main road and the two are joined by an arched bridge (presumably originally the road bridge) which is still passable for cars. There is room for around ten cars on each section.

The walk
Leave the car park through the small gate by the big gate adjacent to the old bridge and marked with a finger post (Public Footpath), and

immediately turn right to climb steeply uphill on a narrow path. This shortly crosses a new plantation, which it enters and leaves through gates in a deer fence which require you to mind your head. Above the plantation the rather eroded path continues to climb steeply, initially through trees, although these are soon left behind as the gradient eases considerably and the path swings left to climb across the flank of the fellside.

Pause on a rocky outcrop to admire the view of Hartsop across the valley, with Brothers Water below and Red Screes and Kirkstone Pass up to the right. Then continue up through the bracken and shortly approach the top of the ridge. At several large, untidy piles of stones, the path swings

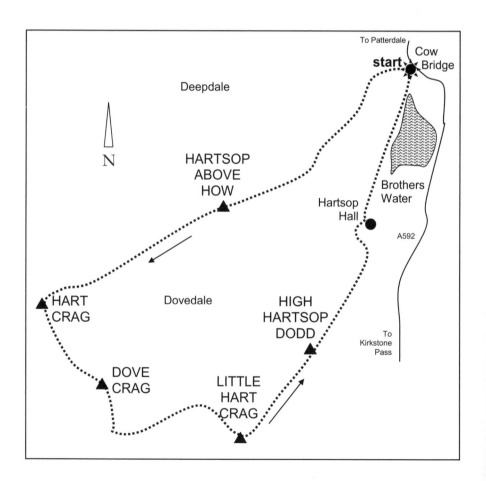

Looking up Kirkstone Pass from the climb to Hartsop above How

left to join a thin path running along the ridge. Continue to climb gently on this; cross a broken wall, and swing right with the path to rise to the ridge-top wall.

Cross the ladder stile and go left with the path to continue to climb the ridge, initially up an easy rocky section. Down on the right is Deepdale with St Sunday Crag beyond; Fairfield is to its left across Grisedale Hause and left of that is our destination – Hart Crag.

Unfolding ahead is a long grassy, undulating ridge, along which the walking is very pleasant. Traverse the first high point, and cross a shallow depression to the summit of Hartsop above How. Here there are a number of outcrops, the furthest of which, which has no cairn or other adornment, and which lies a few yards to the left of the main path, is the highest. From here our onward route is clearly seen – to Hart Crag, left to Dove Crag, and then down the ridge back towards the valley.

So follow the path on across the depression and begin the ascent proper of Hart Crag. This is initially easy but as the ground steepens the path becomes stonier, and an escape to the abundant neighbouring grass is recommended. Soon the gradient eases, the way becomes grassy again, and arrives at the edge of the summit plateau. The path now bends left and then right as it continues up to the skyline and the large cairn which marks the summit of Hart Crag.

Our route has now joined the popular Fairfield Horseshoe (Walk 18) and follows its line for the next few minutes. So leave the summit southwards, picking up the major, and probably quite busy, path which crosses the depression and climbs with a broken wall on its right to the summit of Dove Crag, from where the most extensive view on the walk is obtained. Continue in the same direction, still in company with the broken wall, on easier ground heading directly towards the distant Windermere Lake. In just a couple of minutes, just beyond where the wall swings right, arrive at two piles of stones marking the beginning of a line of old metal fence posts running off to the left. Here turn left to follow an initially indistinct path alongside the fence posts. This quickly becomes very clear and follows the posts down a steeper section, on which it is not hard to circumvent the loose stone. On the left can be seen the ridge along which we ascended, and half right is a rocky lump which is our next destination.

As the ground levels the path becomes less clear, but continue ahead and then swing round right, still following the fence. The path drops down into a dip, now heading directly towards Little Hart Crag, which has a pointy little cairn on it. Approaching the summit the fence posts begin to drop downhill towards Scandale Pass, but our path swings left across their line and then a little hollow before climbing to the cairn.

Leave Little Hart Crag on the thin path which heads east across a depression towards a rocky knoll with a cairn. However, on reaching the lowest point in the depression, turn left down another thin path which begins to descend northwards and then swings right to join a clearer path coming in from the left. Continue on the combined path, which soon swings left and descends easily down the top of the broad grassy ridge towards Brothers Water. The high level section of the ridge ends on High Hartsop Dodd, the "summit" of which is marked with half a dozen stones, and beyond which the ground falls away very much more steeply. Continue on down the lengthy, steep descent to cross a broken wall and a high step stile, escaping onto grass where necessary to avoid steep loose stones. On the final descent down to the barn at the foot of the slope, watch for the zig-zag to the left to circumvent a low crag.

Go through the gap in the wall to the right of the barn, cross the small enclosure, go through the kissing gate (signed Campsite and Patterdale), and follow the grassy track across the field and over Dovedale Beck. Across a second field keep right approaching farm buildings, go through a gate and across a small bridge onto a stony track. Turn right and immediately fork left to go round to the left of Hartsop Hall. Go through the gate and continue on the track which runs along above Brothers Water and, after a mile, returns you directly to the car park.

Walk 24
Almost Helvellyn

This is a quality walk which offers some excellent views of Red Tarn cradled between Striding and Swirral Edges on Helvellyn's glorious eastern face, but does so without negotiating either the roughness and exposure of the Edges themselves, or the crowds which queue up to scramble along them. It also includes a superb arrival at the top of a real pointed mountain. On the final ascent of Catstycam the path is at times steep and loose and it is necessary to pick a good way; otherwise the walking is easy – especially the long descent back to Glenridding.

Summits visited	Catstycam (2917ft/890m) Birkhouse Moor (2356ft/718m)
Start	Glenridding
Distance	7.5 miles/12.25km
Height gain	2580ft/790m
Time	6 hours
Map	OS Explorer OL5 (North-eastern)
Facilities	There are an Information Centre, which is open daily from 0930 to 1730, and toilets on the car park, and shops, cafés and accommodation nearby

Parking: Park in National Park Authority pay and display car park in Glenridding (NY 385170).

The walk

Leave the car park the way you drove in. At the road turn right across the bridge and immediately right again up the tarmac lane beside Glenridding Beck (signed Miresbeck and Helvellyn). At a fork go right (signed Gillside,

Miresbeck, Greenside and Helvellyn) and continue by the beck past the campsite to join a metalled road at Rattlebeck Bridge. Turn left uphill (signed Miresbeck) and immediately fork right off the road onto a narrow path by the wall which quickly joins a wide stony track coming in from the left. Continue up by the wall and at a junction go straight on uphill (signed Helvellyn via Miresbeck). Continue quite steeply up this rough vehicle track and soon arrive at a junction in front of a white gate with a "Private" sign. Here go right with the main walking track, following directions engraved on a vertical slate slab to Greenside and Helvellyn via Miresbeck. The track continues roughly uphill and swings left to a gate/ladder stile inscribed "Helvellyn via Greenhead Mine and Red Tarn". Go over and keep right to walk along the level path above the wall; the left-hand way is our return route.

At a waymarked fork keep right along a virtually level path above the wall on the right and parallel to Glenridding Beck and the old mine road below. At a second fork keep right again on a level course, following the direction of the power lines. The path narrows as it comes opposite a group of restored buildings, with the Youth Hostel to their right and Swart Beck tumbling down the fellside above them. The path rises slightly to join a

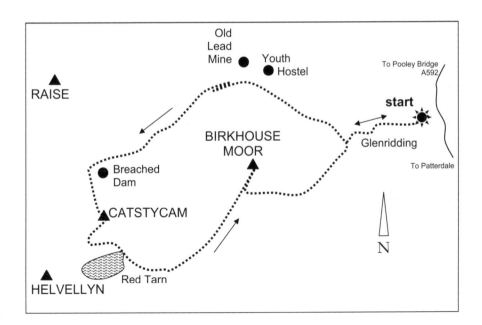

clearer path, and runs on past a small dam (part of Glenridding's hydroelectric scheme), to arrive at a new wooden bridge with an unusual double gate. Cross it, and follow the track which turns right and sets off back down the valley. Then, once past the dam, take the first opportunity to turn sharp left up a little path which climbs diagonally across the fellside, taking us back in the correct direction again. When this peters out, scramble up to the right a few paces to find a grassy track rising up in the same direction. When this also expires, again strike off right uphill to quickly find a wide stony track.

Follow this up the valley directly towards Catstycam, the clear cone of which still looks disconcertingly high and distant. At a fork, where a green track rises right, keep left on the lower way and continue to another fork at the brow of a rise. Here keep left again on the level, grassy way and very shortly see ahead the breached dam in Kepple Cove. Pass the end of the dam and all its warning signs and continue ahead, ignoring the track swinging right. Go past a "No camping in Sheepfolds" sign, and down the

Catstycam and the east face of Helvellyn

outside (left-hand side) of a fenced enclosure. A path descends steeply and roughly the short distance to a rocky ford across the stream; go down this or, preferably, find an easier way down grass on the right. From the ford, climb ahead up the grass bank, pass some ruins on the left and continue along the line of an old water cut to drop on a sketchy path to a second stream.

Cross this at a convenient point and head up the pathless rough grass beyond towards the ridge top, soon swinging left to begin the ascent of the ridge proper. This is a matter of picking an easy way up on grass between stones and small outcrops. A clear path does develop but as this is steepish and quite eroded in the middle section of the climb, it should not be sought too diligently. Towards the top, the path becomes less steep, less stony and more stable and zig-zags pleasantly up to arrive suddenly and dramatically on the pointy top of Catstycam.

The view is good. To the north-east is Ullswater, and to its right, Red Tarn with Striding Edge beyond, the splendid East Wall of Helvellyn and Swirral Edge, the latter three possibly swarming with people, and with queues forming at the trickier bits on both of the edges. From Helvellyn the high ground runs on over White Side and Raise to Sticks Pass and beyond to Great Dodd and Clough Head.

Leave the top on the stony path heading south-west towards Swirral Edge and make the short descent to the depression between Catstycam and Helvellyn. Once on leveller ground, look for an easy way down the grass on the left which avoids the stones and drop down to the path running along by Red Tarn. Turn left onto this path, and where it forks just beyond the tarn, take the right-hand way which doubles back a bit towards the tarn and crosses its outflow (from where there is an opportunity for a short detour to the shore of tarn) before swinging back left. Initially there is a little roughness, but this is soon replaced by a long, level, reconstructed section of path with an excellent surface. The views behind to Helvellyn, Catstycam and the two ridges are pretty good.

Arrive at a ladder stile but do not go over it; instead turn left alongside the wall. Over a rise a view of Ullswater backed by the Pennines opens up ahead. The high point reached before the wall swings away to the right is the summit of Birkhouse Moor and may, or may not, be adorned with a small cairn. However, do not linger here but, for a rather better view down

Ullswater, continue a little way, going straight on along a thin trod where the main path swings right, to reach the prominent cairn at the top of the mountain's north-east ridge.

Return to the main path, and turn left to follow it as it winds easily down, much of it being paved or stepped. Soon Glenridding appears below. Keep on the main path as it joins a wall coming down from the right and then leaves it again and continues to zig-zag down towards the village. The lower, steeper section of the path is entirely stepped, and eventually, having crossed a stream, arrives back at the gate/ladder stile used on the outward route. Turn right downhill to retrace your steps down to Rattlebeck Bridge and through the campsite to follow the stream back to the car park.

Walk 25
Saint Sunday Crag

The steep slopes and tidy elongated summit of St Sunday Crag are prominent features in the landscape of the Ullswater valley and make the mountain an attractive destination. This easy route of ascent, via the complete length of Deepdale, has some excellent mountain scenery and deals with all the steep climbing in one short, sharp section. The summit is reached along one of the finest ridges in Lakeland, and the descent uses the popular direct route back to Patterdale with its classic views of Ullswater.

Summit visited	St Sunday Crag (2756ft/841m)
Start	Patterdale
Distance	7.75 miles/12.5km
Height gain	2300ft/700m
Time	5.5 hours
Map	OS Explorer OL5 (North-eastern)
Facilities	There are toilets, a shop, a pub and a hotel in Patterdale

Parking: The public car park in Patterdale (NY 396159), which belongs to the Patterdale Hotel and operates on a pay and display basis (currently £3.50 per day) is a strangely shaped, often muddy affair. Its entrance is on the left travelling from Glenridding shortly before the entrance to the hotel and is clearly marked with a traditional blue and white sign.

The walk
Leave the car park and turn left to walk south towards Kirkstone Pass on the A592 for 0.75 miles/1.25km, passing the shop and the toilets on the right. There is a pavement on one side of the road or the other, except for a short section just out of the village.

After passing Noran Bank Farm on the right, the road drops and swings left. Just round the first part of this corner, where the pavement ends, a sign advertising B&B at Greenbank Farm and a finger-post (Public Footpath Deepdale) indicate the start of a good track running up the valley on the right. Our route follows this all the way up the valley to its head at Deepdale Hause, 3.25 miles/5.25km distant.

The first two-thirds of the way to the Hause is essentially level. The track initially passes a number of habitations and goes through a farmyard but the way ahead is always clear. Beyond Deepdale Hall, signs of human habitation become scattered and it quickly feels as if people and places have been left behind. After a good 0.75 miles/1.25km, the broad track ends at the metal front gate of Wall End, and the footpath continues as a grassy way, winding on easily up the deepening valley with St Sunday Crag

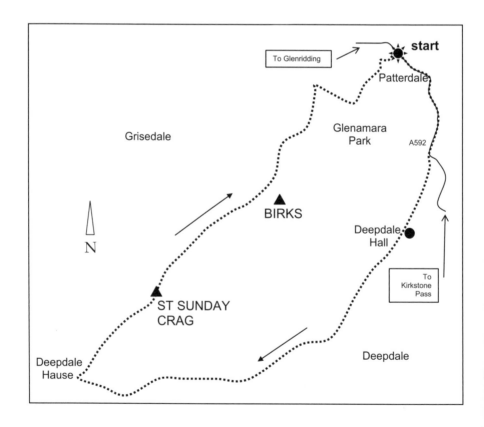

Greenhow End seen on the walk up Deepdale

now on the right and the ground rising to Hart Crag and Fairfield on the left. The path splits a number of times but the two ways always shortly rejoin. As the valley gradually swings round to the right, the dalehead comes into view with some excellent mountain scenery. Its centrepiece is Greenhow End, a line of crags and gullies which are Fairfield's north-east face; to their left is the dip of Link Hause (below which is the hanging valley of Link Cove) leading to the rounded summit of Hart Crag; to their right is a crinkly ridge dropping to Deepdale Hause. Also look back down the valley for a nice view of the twin peaks of Angletarn Pikes.

At last the path begins to climb, and undulates over some moraines, where the previously good view of the crags becomes magnificent! The path rises by cascades with some trees, levels and swings right before climbing easily over and between drumlins, and passing a substantial sheepfold with one square end and one rounded end, to arrive at the foot of the final slope.

The path, now faint at times, initially finds a way to wind up the slope almost exclusively on grass. Then, part way up, the path moves over left and becomes less easy to see as it winds up a ribbon of stones. Continuing on the path is easy at first but the stones become loose and steep and enclosed between two low crags before emerging onto grass as the ridge top is approached; a narrow, shallow grass gully on the right offers an escape from the loose stones but is still steep and may be wet. So instead of moving left with the path, forsake the trodden way and, looking ahead and to the right, choose a good way up the plentiful grass between the low crags.

On reaching the ridge, there suddenly appears an excellent view of the Helvellyn range with Grisedale Tarn below; admire this now as it is not so well seen from the summit. To the right, the ridge to the top of St Sunday Crag beckons irresistibly. Depending on exactly where you gained the ridge top, there may be a minute or two of downhill before you cross the lowest point and recommence the climb. Pass a cairn on the left, which marks the top of the path up from Grisedale, and amble up the delightful ridge to the summit.

The view from the sprawling cairn is good. Notable is the long top of Fairfield with Hart Crag, Dove Crag and Red Screes to its left, and the Langdale and Scafell ranges to its right. Ullswater is not seen well from here but will become a fine picture on the descent.

Leave the top east of north (in the general direction of Ullswater) to find a developing path heading towards some prominent cairns and a rocky outcrop. From here the path briefly drops half-left before swinging back right to descend to a prominent cairn on an edge; this marks the classic viewpoint of Ullswater. The path goes to the left of the cairn and, still heading towards the lake, drops to another rocky outcrop, before continuing clearly down; the views of the lake continue to be glorious.

The way is briefly steeper and stonier but it is not hard to find an easy route down. Then at the foot of the slope there is a fork; here keep left on the clearer path which initially contours round the fellside, and then drops easily with good views across the valley to Birkhouse Moor. The path crosses a stile in a wall and immediately goes left to initially descend parallel to the wall before swinging right and commencing a stepped section which continues almost to the valley bottom. Here the path approaches a cross-fence with two gates, a large metal one and a small wooden one. Use neither, but instead turn right and follow the clear path which runs along above the fence. Follow this round the contour, ignoring a green path which strikes off uphill, cross a stream on stepping stones, go through a kissing gate by a big gate, and descend to a kissing gate leading into a wooded area. Go through and quickly arrive at a fork, where you go left for a direct return to the car park through the grounds of the Patterdale Hotel. But if you need to return via the toilets, shop or White Lion pub, go right instead, turning right again at the unmade track to pass the toilets on the right and emerge onto the main road with the shop and pub on the left. Go left for the car park.

Walk 26
High Street and its neighbours

An easy high level circuit of Riggindale which traverses the Far Eastern Fells' best ridge, and visits their highest top and most distinctive summit. There is also an encounter with a Roman Road, and some pretty good views.

Summits visited	Rough Crag (2060ft/628m) High Street (2718ft/828m) Rampsgill Head (2598ft/792m) Kidsty Pike (2560ft/780m) With an optional extension to High Raise (2633ft/802m)
Start	Mardale Head
Distance	7.25 miles/11.5km
Height gain	2340ft/710m
Time	5.5 hours
Map	OS Explorer OL5 (North-eastern)
Facilities	There is a shop with a tea room, and a pub in Bampton

Including the extension to High Raise adds 0.75 miles/1.25km, 250ft/80m of ascent and 0.5 hours to the walk.

Parking: Park at the head of Haweswater (NY 469107) where there is room for a total of around two dozen cars in a car park and spaces marked on the adjacent road. If all this is full, there are a couple of small roadside spaces nearby, but there is a consensus that the road hereabouts, constructed when the valley was flooded, is wide enough for parking on the road itself.

The walk

Leave the parking area at the road end through the kissing gate by the old but well maintained MCWW (Manchester Corporation Water Works) signpost. The sign also claims to be a bus stop, although a nearby notice points out that the nearest real bus stop is in Burnbanks, 5 miles/8km back up the valley.

Through the gate, almost immediately a junction with a short finger-post and a choice of three onward ways is reached. Here go right, (signed Bampton), and follow the repaired path across the valley above the head of the lake. Our route to the summit of High Street lies leftwards along the crest of the ridge ahead but a short detour right is necessary to gain the ridge top. So, approaching the far side of the water, after crossing the wide wooden footbridge spanning Mardale Beck, go right with the main track which continues above the lake shore. Shortly, a useful short cut up

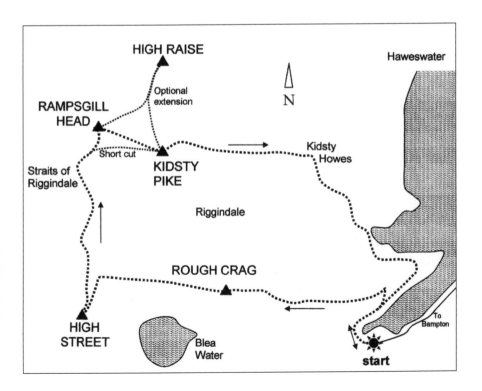

onto the ridge will be found climbing steeply half-left opposite a wall corner. Though initially rough, the way soon improves and quickly arrives at a junction of paths at a cairn close to the top of the ridge.

Go left past a plethora of cairns of various sizes and follow the path as it ambles its way up the ridge, sometimes near to its crest and sometimes on a slightly lower course on its left-hand flank. Higher up, the very pleasant path settles on a line close to the top of the wide grassy ridge, and then, as a corner is rounded, the summit plateau of High Street comes into view. To its left are Mardale Ill Bell and Harter Fell, whilst on its right is seen our onward route round the head of Riggindale, over Kidsty Pike and down the long, high grassy ridge back towards Haweswater. The two tarns which appear on the left, are Blea Water immediately below, and Small Water beyond.

Soon a high point on the ridge looms ahead. Climbing over its top, a second, slightly higher hump appears, and behind that a third yet higher hump, which finally is the top of Rough Crag. From here the summit plateau of High Street looks not too far away. So, continue on the easy path across the depression, past a small tarn, and up the ridge of Long Stile towards the cairn on the skyline. The path makes an easy way up a delightful rocky stairway, and the ridge, which narrows as it approaches the cairn, is an absolutely splendid approach to the top of the mountain. The final section of the path approaching the cairn is covered with loose stone but elsewhere is grass.

The cairn marks the edge of the summit plateau and cannot be passed without pausing for breath and admiring the view back down the full length of Haweswater to the dam with the long, long line of the Pennines beyond. Resume by going half-left past the cairn on the skyline to the broken wall which crosses the summit, and then going left with it for one minute to reach the triangulation column marking the summit of High Street. From here, in clear weather, the view is glorious. Particular gems are the Scafells and Great Gable in the west, the whole of the Helvellyn massif, and the long view south to the estuaries of Morecambe Bay and beyond.

Leave the top north-eastwards, walking with the wall on your right, and follow the path as it descends easily to the Straits of Riggindale. On the left, Hayeswater appears, and the Roman Road, which has crossed the summit plateau west of the highest point, can be seen coming in to join us. Cross the Straits, moving over to the right of the wall for an excellent view down into Riggindale, and almost immediately arrive at a fork marked with a large cairn. Here go right to walk above Twopenny Crag on a path with rises slightly as it swings round the head of the valley. Approaching an area of stones near the top of the rise, the path forks again. The right-hand way goes directly to Kidsty Pike and our return route, but if visibility is good, go left to the cairn which can be seen just ahead and which is the summit of Rampsgill Head, continuing a further 50yds half-left to a second cairn which, totally unexpectedly, stands on the edge of an abrupt declivity and commands a dramatic prospect of the valley of Ramps Gill below. Hallin Fell is prominent at the foot of the valley with two small sections of Ullswater visible either side of it; the other small section of water round to the left is a part of Brothers Water. Return the few paces to the summit cairn.

The main walk now heads directly to Kidsty Pike, the distinctive top of which is visible just south of east. To reach it simply head off in its general direction across easy grass to rejoin the clear path used previously, and follow it on its virtually level course to the shapely top. However, for those collecting summits, High Raise may now also be added to the day's tops with little extra effort. Its summit is visible on the horizon and is reached by continuing along the path north-eastwards across the depression, keeping right to the summit as the stony area at the top of the slope is reached. There is a sprawling cairn and a shelter and a view which, whilst extensive in all directions, doesn't add a great deal to those already seen today. To continue to Kidsty Pike, return to the depression and keep left to follow a clear path which does a beeline diagonally across to its clearly visible top.

Kidsty Pike has a cairn perched on the edge of the declivity falling into Riggindale. The view is restricted by the hills we have visited, but the Coniston and Scafell groups are good, as is the vista of the Solway, complete with many turbines. Those who make a point of looking for the shapely peak of Kidsty Pike from the M6, may like to try it the other way round!

Leave the top north-eastwards to rejoin the very clear and well graded path which heads off south of east to descend the ridge, partly on grass, but mostly resurfaced. In due course the gradient steepens at Kidsty

Howes and the combination of loose stones and the gradient make the path awkward. Here use the adjacent grass slope and then the alternate grass path running down to the left. Once the two ways have merged again, the going becomes easier as the final section of the descent is reached. Continue down, trending left towards the bottom to go round a bog, to arrive at the lake shore path by a little stone bridge which crosses a small stream by some little waterfalls. Turn right and follow the path over a footbridge and across the bottom of Riggindale, from where we may stop and contemplate, with more than a little satisfaction, the route just completed. Continue through some trees, round the end of the ascent ridge, and through a broken wall. The car park is now in sight and, shortly passing the foot of the path climbed this morning, we can simply retrace our steps to the car.

The view back down over Long Stile and Rough Crag

Walk 27
Crummock Water shore
and Rannerdale Knotts

All mountain walks from Buttermere are good, but most are long and strenuous. This is a little gem which in only three miles combines a lakeside perambulation with a visit to a grand little summit with excellent views over the valley. The outward section of the walk makes use of a new permissive path along the south-eastern shore of Crummock Water before tackling the uphill – which is short and sharp and mostly on a beautifully constructed stone staircase. The return route runs along the airy ridge of the fell before making an easy grassy descent back to the village.

Summit visited	Rannerdale Knotts (1165ft/355m)
Start	Buttermere Village
Distance	3 miles/4.75km
Height gain	850ft/260m
Time	2 hours
Map	OS Explorer OL4 (North-western)
Facilities	There are toilets, hotels and seasonal cafés in the village

Parking: Park in the National Trust pay and display car park on the western edge of Buttermere village (NY 173172). Approaching from Lorton on the B5289, the car park is on the right 0.25 miles before the village centre.

The walk
Leave the car park through the kissing gate into Long How woodland (National Trust sign). Turn left at the T-junction and follow the path down through the woodland to Mill Beck. Continue, with the stream on

your left, to a wooden footbridge over it. Cross the bridge and a stile, and turn right (signed Crummock Lake Shore only) to walk along beside the fence.

Where the fence turns right, go with it and follow the path over a wooded knoll and down to the stony shore of Crummock Water. Turn right through a kissing gate and walk half-right to cross a wooden footbridge, continuing to another kissing gate close to the water. Go through this, cross a plank bridge, pass a small stone jetty and immediately fork left (National Trust waymark) to climb a clear stony path through trees. Exit the area of trees through a kissing gate and turn left to descend a grassy slope. Cross a slab bridge and continue parallel to the water to reach another kissing gate. Go through this and continue straight on up to and across the road. Climb the bank opposite and turn left onto a broad green path which rises very gradually above and parallel to the road. The path

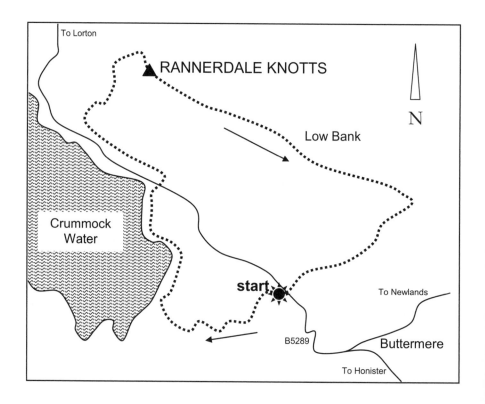

quickly traverses a little rise with exposed rock from where you can see the path rising ahead to pass to the right of a rocky outcrop on the near skyline. 90yds before it reaches this outcrop turn right onto a clear grassy path which runs steeply up the fellside, continuing straight on where the gradient eases on a thin stony path. Looking back, the view of lakes and mountains is now becoming impressive.

The way shortly becomes grassy again and soon arrives at a large low pile of stones at the foot of some scree. Go to the right of this pile of stones and find a thin path which heads up into an area of scree and stones which looks horrible – but turns out to be quite straightforward. For after only a few strides, the path arrives at the foot of a beautifully constructed stone staircase, on which the bulk of the remaining climbing is done. Above the top of the steps the way continues steeply upwards on grass towards some low crags, at the foot of which the path goes right.

The gradient soon eases and the path then swings round to the right as it begins its final climb to the summit. Go up the rocky stairway and fork left up the short grassy slope to arrive a few feet to the left of what clearly appears to be the summit of Rannerdale Knotts – although others think the top is 20yds further on and have built a cairn there. The panorama of high mountains seen from the summit, scanning round to the right from the north-east, includes Grasmoor, Whiteless Pike, Robinson (with High Snockrigg in front of it), Fleetwith Pike, Haystacks, High Crag, High Stile, Red Pike, Starling Dodd, Great Borne and Melbreak.

Leave the top south-eastwards past the cairn, with Crummock Water and Buttermere on the right, to pick up a path which heads off along the ridge gently losing height. The path shortly prefers the right hand side of the ridge crest and thus gives excellent views of the two lakes with Buttermere village between them. There is a rocky step down, which is not difficult, and then the pleasant path descends easily, mostly on grass. Further on, as the ridge nears its end, paths fork off firstly right and then, a little beyond, left, but continue ahead to traverse a small hump and arrive at a clear crosspaths.

Turn right and follow the clear, broad green path down, preferring the right-hand way where there is a choice, to descend to pass to the left of some trees. Continue down into a rushy hollow, swinging left to go round the left-hand side of the wetness, and then rising slightly between rocky

The Buttermere valley from near the summit

outcrops. Keep right at the fork and very soon the car park appears ahead. The path goes left to loose a final bit of height and then turns right to run alongside a walled enclosure to a stile which gives access to the road exactly opposite the car park entrance.

Walk 28
Hard Knott

Hard Knott is a fell of only moderate height and appearance, but one which deserves to be far better known on account of its excellent views of the Scafell range and the other fine hills encircling the head of Eskdale. The ascent takes in an exploration of the extensive remains of the Roman Fort with which the fell shares its name, before following an interesting and scenic route to the summit. The return is an extended loop which descends the hill's pleasant northern ridge into the heart of Upper Eskdale, and continues alongside the picturesque pools and waterfalls of Lingcove Beck and the upper reaches of the River Esk. A clear day is needed for this walk both to fully appreciate the views of the highest ground in England, and also to easily navigate the described route.

Summit visited	Hard Knott (1803ft/549m)
Start	Head of Eskdale at the foot of Hardknott Pass
Distance	5 miles/8km
Height gain	1750ft/530m
Time	4.5 hours plus time to explore the fort
Map	OS Explorer OL6 (South-western)
Facilities	None nearby; the Woolpack Inn is 1.5 miles/2.5km down Eskdale

Parking: At the head of Eskdale, shortly after the road begins to climb Hardknott Pass, there is a cattle grid, and, immediately above this on the right, a parking space for 6-8 cars (NY 214011). If this is full (if necessary there is room to turn round), there are three separate lengths of wide grass verge on the southern side of the road just west of the foot of the pass.

The walk

Walk up the road, ignoring a ladder stile on the left and shortcutting the hairpin bend, to the corner where the wall turns left. Here, marked by a short "Public Footpath" finger-post, a clear green path sets off alongside the wall and soon arrives at Hardknott Castle, a Roman Fort, the remains of which are sufficiently well preserved and well labelled to make a leisurely exploration well worthwhile.

Leave the fort through its north-west gate (on the left relative to the point of arrival) and follow the path round right. Immediately there is an excellent view across to Scafell and Scafell Pike. There are a number of little paths heading off parallel to the edge that drops down into Eskdale on the left; all join up. The path is a bit intermittent in places but the way climbs clearly round to the right of Yew Crag to arrive in a flatter, wetter area where it disappears. Go ahead to a broken wall, pausing to look back at the view down the valley. Climb through the wall at an obvious crossing place and carry on 50yds uphill, still on pathless, wet ground, to a low, vertical rock face. Facing the rock, look right and see a broad, mostly grassy swath with a few rocks here and there, bounded by low crags on its left-hand side and a drop down towards the fort on its right-hand side, rising towards the highest point on the skyline. Choose a way up this; having circumvented the initial wet section, the gradient is easier on the right. Soon a broad grass shelf is reached and running along it, right to left, will be found a clear shepherd's track/sheep trod.

Turn left and follow it north-eastwards, continuing ahead where it becomes indistinct on wet ground. Soon a point is reached at which the view of Upper Eskdale with its encircling mountains (Esk Pike, Bowfell and Crinkle Crags) opens up, with the confluence of the River Esk and Lingcove Beck, past which lies our return route, clearly seen below and slightly left. Directly ahead of us our onward way runs on, heading towards Eskdale Needle – a flat-topped pinnacle marginally higher than our current position. Seen from this angle, the needle stands in front of the crag of which it was once a part and, although only around 300yds away, can be tricky to make out.

Continue, still heading north-eastwards, on the thin path towards the Needle, crossing a broad, shallow gully running up the fellside. As we progress, the Needle becomes more obviously detached from the rocks behind it. The thin path leads to a wide, shallow grass gully to the right of the Needle, across which runs a broken wall. Cross the wall and continue up the grass slope beyond, heading for what looks like a pile of stones above. Then when the gradient eases, and you reach the stones (which turn out to be some scattered rocks rather than a constructed cairn), turn right to head up a broad grass gully, climbing fairly steeply

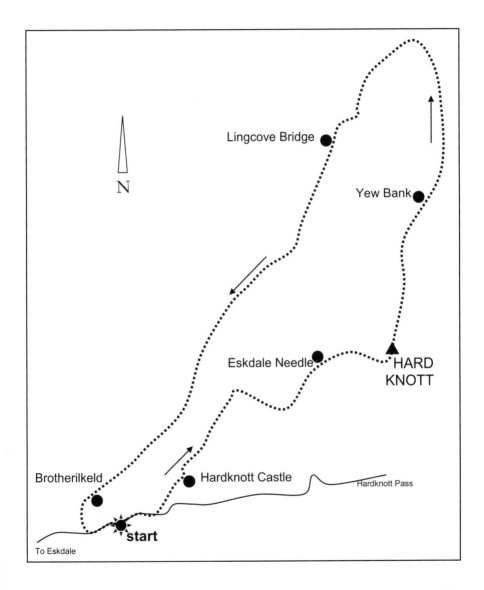

close to the foot of two low crags on the left. Where the gradient eases, continue ahead a short distance to find a disused electric fence. Turn left along the fence, stepping over it at some convenient point onto a path which leads to the top of some rocks on which is perched a shapely cairn with a wonderful view; this is the summit of Hard Knott.

Head off from the summit on a narrow path running northwards towards the head of Eskdale. The little path winds down and comes back into company with the fence. A clear path now runs parallel to the fence, descending easily to cross it at a stile and continue alongside it. The thin path crosses a rather wet, shallow depression and passes to the right of a cairned high point before arriving at a fork. The right-hand branch goes to another stile in the old fence, but keep left to remain on the left of the fence on a good path. Care may be necessary to avoid stray strands of wire from the old fence. Ignore a further stile on the right as the way continues gently down on grass, still parallel to the fence. Despite the loss

In upper Eskdale; Lingcove Bridge spans Lingcove Beck at its confluence with the River Esk

of height, it could be argued that the scenery gets better as you approach the head of the valley; the path comes quite close to the slopes of Crinkle Crags, which now rises up or our right, as it approaches the stream (Lingcove Beck) draining down from below Bowfell, ahead.

Continue ahead, maintaining direction and noting that the fence has drifted away from us over on the right, and drop onto a grass path which has come down from a gate in the fence. Turn left to walk directly towards Mickledore, the gash separating Scafell from Scafell Pike – another fine sight. The path drops gently, swinging left at a bouldery area to drop down to run to the left of the beck which will guide us back to Brotherilkeld. A clear path comes in from the right and the combined way continues to drop gently with the beck tumbling down on our right.

Rounding a left-hand bend, the view ahead opens up, with our return route running on besides the water below, and Eskdale beyond. Shortly, the photogenic stone arch of Lingcove Bridge can be picked out, just this side of a sheepfold, spanning the beck close to its confluence with the River Esk. The rocky section of the path leading down to the bridge needs to be taken slowly and with care. Just above the bridge, a detour right of a few paces is rewarded with a good view of a nice waterfall. This is a delightful spot.

Continue still with the water on the right, now on a very much easier, virtually level path. Cross the wall using a ladder stile and follow the onward path as it drops half-right down the field and winds across pastures, passing through a cross-wall at a gate. Soon the farm buildings at Brotherilkeld come into view and at a pair of gates, signs direct us through the smaller one and along to the right of a fence to walk besides the river. Ignore a wooden footbridge on the right and continue through a kissing gate and over a sleeper bridge to join the farm access track; turn right to emerge onto the metalled road at the red phone box exactly at the foot of Hardknott Pass.

Walk 29
The hills of Nether Wasdale

The hills that are first encountered approaching Wasdale from Gosforth, whilst not having the altitude and grandeur of those surrounding the head of the valley, also present interesting steep and stony faces to the arriving visitor and offer from their summits big panoramas which extend from the highest mountains in the land to the sandy beaches of West Cumbria. And, as a real bonus, they offer the opportunity to visit those summits on easy paths which are almost entirely grassy and well-graded. Then, without travelling too far, a perfect day can be rounded off with a walk by the sea at Seascale as the sun sinks gloriously towards the horizon.

Summits visited	Middle Fell (1908ft/582m) Seatallan (2266ft/691m) Glade How (1420ft/433m) Buckbarrow (1410ft/430m)
Start	Greendale
Distance	6.75 miles/10.75km
Height gain	2450ft/750m
Time	5.25 hours
Map	OS Explorer OL6 (South-western)
Facilities	The nearest hotel/inn is at Nether Wasdale. Gosforth, 5.25 miles/8.5km from Greendale, has toilets, shops and a good choice of eating places and accommodation

Parking: Park towards the foot of Wasdale, at Greendale (NY 144056). Approaching from Gosforth, immediately beyond Greendale hamlet there is plenty of parking space on a wide verge on the left, plus room for an extra couple of cars on the right. If this is full, further towards the lake there is plenty of space on the right beyond the end of the wall.

The walk

A finger post by the road indicates a clear way that climbs the hillside with Middle Fell on the right and Buckbarrow on the left. Of the two ways up the slope, choose the original right hand path which is less steep, and, having been repaired, is easier underfoot. At the top of the slope, where the path swings right to run high above Greendale Gill, fork right on a grassy way which climbs up the shoulder of Middle Fell. This path zig-zags easily and pleasantly up the ridge, generally preferring a line slightly right of the ridge top. Approaching the highest point, many small paths continue uphill; all lead to the summit cairn.

From the top of Middle Fell the view is excellent, with the Scafell massif looking particularly magnificent. To its left is Great Gable with Yewbarrow in front of it, and then, on the near skyline, Kirk Fell, Red Pike, Haycock and Seatallan with its broad ridge, which we shall descend, running down to Buckbarrow. To the right of the Scafells is the full length of Wastwater,

Wastwater and the Scafell massif from Middle Fell

with Illgill Head and Whin Rigg behind, and further round to the west an extensive view seaward from Black Coombe to Sellafield with the sandy estuary at Ravenglass taking centre stage.

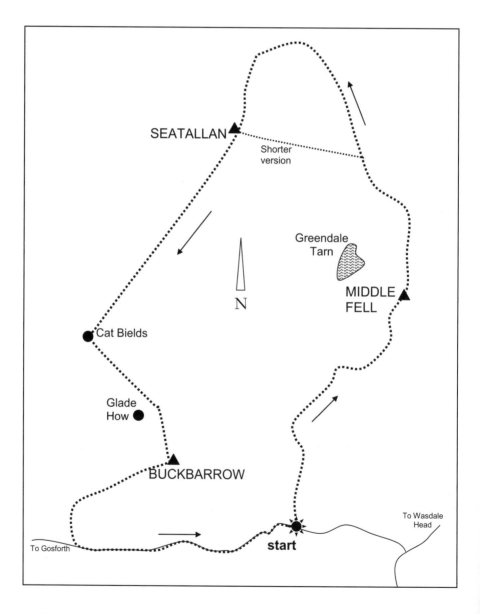

Leave the summit on either of the two paths which set off west of north and drop down the slopes of Middle Fell towards Seatallan. During this descent, two major paths are clearly seen below in the depression; the first continues in the current direction of travel and runs right of the main bulk of Seatallan to rise to the right of a rocky knoll, and the second goes left from the depression and heads directly for the top, but fades when it reaches steeper ground. The latter direct path could be taken to reach the summit more quickly, but our main route prefers the former option which, at the cost of only an extra 0.5 miles/1km, includes a pleasant perambulation high on the slopes above Nether Beck and a less arduous final climb.

Continue into the spongy depression between Middle Fell and Seatallan, from where three paths diverge. Take the right-hand one, which heads north round the right-hand flank of Seatallan, climbing to the right of some low crags and continuing clearly round the contour. On the right, across Nether Beck, the slopes rise to Wasdale's Red Pike. Continue on the narrow way until, having left the crags behind, you arrive at a point at which the path trends right and begins to drop. Here strike off half-left across pathless territory towards the ridge ahead, up which will be found rising the ridge path coming across from Haycock. Turn left up it, and where it peters out as it approaches the top of the steep ground, continue ahead past a cairn to quickly arrive at the large, ancient cairn and trigonometric column on the summit. Seatallan being a mountain with a broad, flat summit plateau, this is not a particularly good viewpoint, but the promontories on its southern edge, which we are to visit on our return, are.

Set off due south from the OS column, picking up one of the three parallel tracks. These quickly disappear on short cropped turf, but maintain direction and a path soon reappears and continues down gently-sloping grass heading for the distant cairn on Cat Bields – which is visible from the summit in clear conditions.

At Cat Bields, turn left on a path which shortly begins to fall a little more steeply before crossing a marshy section. It then rises left of a very neat, prominent cairn before swinging right to visit it. This is Glade How. Looking out to sea, Buckbarrow is on the left, its cairn silhouetted against the Screes across Wastwater. Leave on one of the two paths heading off south-east (the left-hand one probably being slightly drier and easier) and arrive at the summit of Buckbarrow – a high point on the long ridge falling from Seatallan. From here, 180yds in the same direction (south-south-east) towards the Screes and across a depression, is a further cairn sitting on the edge of the summit plateau; make your way across to it using one of the many paths for an excellent view of the Screes, of nearly all of Wastwater, and of the car parked at Greendale below.

Start the descent as if returning to Buckbarrow summit, but at the lowest point in the depression turn left on a thin but clear trod heading towards the sea. The path drops pleasantly on grass, heading in the direction of Sellafield, and disappearing over what appears to be the edge of a steep drop. However, on arriving at the "edge", it transpires that the path runs on easily beyond it and continues pleasantly down, crossing one stream and running for a time alongside another. At one point the path becomes very rough and needs to be circumvented, but it quickly improves again. In due course the path zig-zags its way down a little stonily towards trees and soon arrives in a wooded area and then at the tarmac road. Go left and walk for 20 minutes back to the car, noting on the left the line of crags which have made it necessary to follow this circuitous route back to our starting point.

Walk 30
The Loweswater Fells

Tucked away in the north-west corner of Lakeland are a group of grassy hills of modest height which provide some easy, quiet walking with good views of both high mountains and the sea. This walk to three of their summits uses well-trodden tracks at low level, and narrow but generally clear paths on the hills. There is a short pathless section on ascent, but in clear weather there are no problems with route finding.

Summits visited	Carling Knott (1785ft/544m) Blake Fell (1878ft/573m) Gavel Fell (1726ft/526m)
Start	Maggie's Bridge
Distance	6.25 miles/10km
Height gain	1820ft/550m
Time	4.5 hours
Map	OS Explorer OL4 (North-western)
Facilities	The Kirkstile Inn is beside Loweswater church, 0.5 miles/0.75km from the parking area

Parking: Park on the small National Trust car park at Maggie's Bridge (NY 135210). Travelling on the B5289 from Lorton, where the road to Buttermere goes off left, go straight on towards Loweswater. After a further 1.5 miles/2.5km, beyond two lane-ends with brown "Kirkstile Inn" signs, on the left is a narrow, tarmac lane with a finger post ("Public Bridleway Loweswater 0.8 miles") which leads to the parking area by Maggie's Bridge.

The walk

Leave the car park through the gate by the cattle grid and walk along the farm road towards the lake. Approaching Watergate Farm branch right on a grassy way; go through the gate into Holme Wood and immediately turn left on a path climbing through the trees. Continue to climb steadily through the wood, ignoring all cross paths, to reach a kissing gate. Here leave the wood and in a few strides arrive at a broad green bridleway running round the hillside above the lake. Turn left onto this gently rising way and continue, with views across the Solway opening up behind, to a

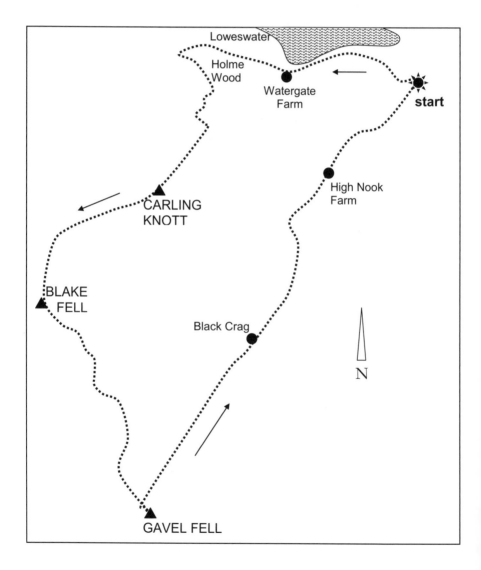

gate at its highest point. Go through, and immediately turn right to climb alongside the fence, although initially it may be helpful to detour briefly away from the fence to negotiate the easiest way through a band of bracken. Soon, when low crags bar the way, fork left to climb steeply up the bilberry covered slope between two trees. Above these you will find a clear sheep-track which runs round the contour; turn right onto this and follow it to the top of the crag. Here admire the view (which will become less good as the summit plateau is reached) before striking uphill, following bits and pieces of a trod through thickish bilberry, and trending slightly left to find the well-built cairn on the end of Carling Knott.

Leave the cairn on the narrow but clear trod heading south-west which quickly arrives on the flat summit of Carling Knott, where there are several piles of stones and a substantial shelter marking the highest point.

Our next objective, Blake Fell, is now in view, and a thin but clear path heads off towards it, running along the top of a low line of crags and crossing a depression before climbing its slopes. Follow this, crossing the fence at a step stile and continuing for two minutes beyond to the substantial cairn on the summit. From this vantage point close to the north-western boundary of the National Park, on a clear day the view is good in all directions. Westwards, beyond Cogra Moss Reservoir, are the coast, the sea and the mountains of Scotland, and eastwards is a splendid panorama of the mountains of Lakeland. The glimpse of Buttermere cradled by fine mountains is a real gem.

Leave the top of Blake Fell on the clear path running south-east. This quickly comes alongside a fence (do not cross the stile) and descends with it past the ruins of a sheepfold, short-cutting across a right-hand corner, to arrive at a junction of fences. Here, go over the stile and walk down the slope with the fence on your right to another stile. Go over and follow the narrow path to where it meets a broader one; turn left and climb with it across the slope to meet the fence at a corner. The path then climbs with the fence, and continues to the summit of Gavel Fell, which is marked with a neat cairn.

To start the easy, grassy descent, first return a short distance to the first fence junction. Here cross the first stile, and follow the thin but clear path which sets off north-eastwards, diagonally across the space between the two fences. Continue on this path as it crosses a marshy depression before rising to a prominent cairn and then running on along the broad ridge towards Black Crag, preferring the right fork at any bifurcations. The thin path drops off the end of the ridge and swings right to join an old bridleway; go left. The track drops to join a path coming in from the left, goes through a gate, and continues down and through the buildings of High Nook Farm. Walk down the farm's access road, ignoring a ladder stile on the left, and arrive at Maggie's Bridge, which takes you over Dub Beck, the outflow from Loweswater, to the parking area.

Buttermere and Fleetwith Pike glimpsed from Blake Fell

Walk 31
The best views; Honister to Green Gable

Whilst nearly all walks to Lakeland summits reward with good views, this excursion offers vistas that are truly exceptional, and the possibility of taking photographs which are award-winning. This is a walk which really must be done on a clear, bright day. The route described is most commonly used as an approach to Great Gable, but although visiting three tops, it stops short of the final section to avoid some rough terrain. The walk also has the advantage of starting at an elevation of 1175ft/360m, with the bulk of the remaining climbing being dealt with in an initial short sharp section. What then follows is a fine high level expedition with easy walking. Whilst included in the 'Western' section of the book, the walk is also easily accessible from bases in the Keswick area.

Summits visited	Grey Knotts (2287ft/697m) Brandreth (2344ft/715m) Green Gable (2628ft/801m)
Start	Honister Pass
Distance	5.75 miles/9km
Height gain	1700ft/520m
Time	4.75 hours
Map	OS Explorer OL4 (North-western)
Facilities	A large sign indicates the location of a unisex "daytime toilet" at the back of the hostel. The Honister Slate Mine complex is adjacent to the car park and has limited refreshment facilities within its visitor reception area

Parking: Park in the National Trust pay and display car park at the top of Honister Pass (NY 225135). Approaching from Buttermere, its entrance is

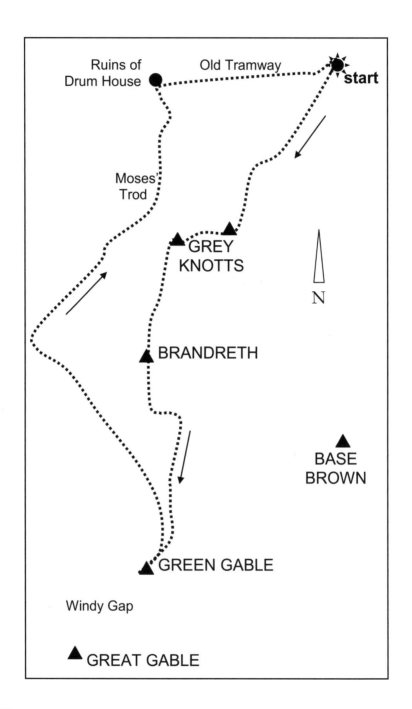

Ruins of
Drum House

Old Tramway

start

Moses'
Trod

GREY
KNOTTS

N

BRANDRETH

BASE
BROWN

GREEN GABLE

Windy Gap

GREAT GABLE

on the right immediately after the Youth Hostel. There is space for around 30 cars.

The walk

Leave the car park from its south-western corner through the gate signed "Footpath to Grey Knotts". Walk across the mine working area, exiting it by a step stile and heading up the path which climbs steeply alongside the fence. This is pitched and paved all the way up to the initial skyline, where the gradient eases. Continue to climb with the fence on your right, now on rougher ground. The ground steepens again and becomes more stony; options to detour away from the fence are recommended.

Above this second steeper section cross one of the two step stiles in the fence and continue uphill, now with the fence on your left. Shortly the fence and path turn right and quickly arrive at another step stile. Go over it. Immediately half right is a rock outcrop, which is the eastern summit of Grey Knotts. To reach its cairn easily, continue a little way alongside the fence and tackle the outcrop from its far (western) side.

Return to the fence and continue the few paces to where it turns left. Climb the wooden hurdle and follow the path which sets off half-left and wanders to Grey Knott's western summit. The view is stunning. Centre stage are the lakes of Buttermere and Crummock Water; to their right is Fleetwith Pike, and to their left Haystacks and the High Stile ridge; left again is Ennerdale, then Pillar, Kirk Fell and Great Gable.

Leave the cairn on the thin path which sets off southwards and winds across the hollow in the direction of Brandreth. Cross a step stile by a fence corner and continue ahead up the stony slope following the line of old metal fence posts. The views over to the right continue to be brilliant. Where the ground levels as the summit of Brandreth is reached, pass a cairn on your left and continue forward. Ahead is a cairn with a metal post in it which marks the line of our path, and to its left a cairn which probably marks the highest point.

Continue slightly left, heading now towards the top of the aptly named Green Gable, and pick up a faint trod which generally follows the line of the old posts. Part way down the slope, reach a path which is a not very clear on the ground but is extraordinarily well cairned, and comes in from behind you on the right and continues half left. Turn left onto it. The

Ennerdale framed between Pillar and the High Stile ridge

route ahead now is clear – down to the left of some small tarns and then right across the depression and up the slope of Green Gable opposite. Beyond the depression the Seathwaite Valley appears down on the left with Base Brown rising beyond it. Arriving at the summit of Green Gable, the rocky cone of Great Gable appears dramatically across Windy Gap.

Leave the top by retracing steps down the broad stony path dropping on grass. Before arriving at the bottom of the initial slope, there is a fork; go left to remain on our outward route. Ahead there is a rocky outcrop which our path passes on its left; when opposite the outcrop fork left off the path to head just west of north towards the distant Skiddaw. In front of Skiddaw you will see Moses Trod, a clear wide path running over a grassy shoulder, and, coming in to join it from below on the right, a less wide path – which we are going to pick up. So, continue down, keeping just left of the boulder fields and rocky outcrops which run down the crest of the ridge, and you will find a trod, which gradually becomes clearer and, still running west of north, drops to pick up another line of old fence posts. Approaching the depression there is a fork, the left branch of which is the path seen from above; advance on it to Moses Trod and keep right on the gently rising path.

[In poor visibility, retrace steps all the way down the slope to the depression with the small tarns. If things have improved here, turn left just before the first piece of water and head north of west, as if heading down Ennerdale, cross a narrow cross-trod, go half-right on a clear path and keep right to reach Moses Trod. Otherwise continue past the tarns on the outward way and remain on the clearly cairned way.]

On the left the rock architecture of Great Gable, Kirk Fell and Pillar is magnificent, and for completeness, there is a glimpse of the Irish Sea over Beck Head. At the top of the rise (which is the watershed between Ennerdale and Buttermere), is a fence with two step stiles. Keep right and cross the top one from which there is a brilliant view down Buttermere. Advance from the stile to quickly meet a broad stony track and turn left on to it. The track shortly swings right and runs on, having been joined from the left by a path coming up from Ennerdale, to meet an old tramway above Honister at the foundations of the former Drum House. Turn right and, with Borrowdale beneath your boots, walk back down to the mine buildings. At the bottom of the track, cross the mine area and walk between the buildings to reach the gate into the car park.

Walk 32
Grasmoor

A direct ascent of Grasmoor, the highest of the north-western hills, is followed by some good high level walking on clear paths and a straightforward descent. The scenery is excellent throughout with the bonus of a fine finish through a blue carpet if the walk is done at bluebell time. A shorter version of walk is described but is recommended only as an escape from deteriorating weather. Crag Hill, as it is known to the Ordnance Survey, is given its alternative name of Eel Crag by Wainwright.

Summits visited	Grasmoor (2795ft/852m) Crag Hill (2752ft/839m) Wandope (2533ft/772m) Thirdgill Head Man (2402ft/732m) Whiteless Pike (2165ft/660m) A shorter version omits Crag Hill and Wandope
Start	Cinderdale Common
Distance	7.25 miles/11.75km
Height gain	3080ft/940m
Time	5.75 hours
Map	OS Explorer OL4 (North-western)
Facilities	In Buttermere village there are toilets, an Inn, a Hotel and seasonal cafés

These figures reduce to 6 miles/9.5km, 2540ft/770m and 5.25 hours if the shorter option is taken.

Parking: Park at Cinderdale Common (NY 162193), which is 2 miles/3.25km north-west of Buttermere on the B5289. There are two equally convenient parking areas, each with room for 10/12 cars.

The walk

From the more northerly of the two parking areas, walk on grass, following the road towards Buttermere, to the more southerly one. Walk up by the stream the short distance to where a track fords it, cross the water and continue up the other bank.

The path climbs easily, at first beside the stream and then rising above it onto a rocky knoll. Above this the grassy path swings right to leave the stream and wind pleasantly up on the well-defined ridge which separates Crummock Water on the right from the valley of Cinderdale Beck on the left, and shortly arrives at Lad Hows, a small swelling on the ridge. Ahead is the ridge from Thirdgill Head Man over Whiteless Pike, along which lies our route of descent, whilst behind has opened up a panorama stretching from the coast round to the Scafells.

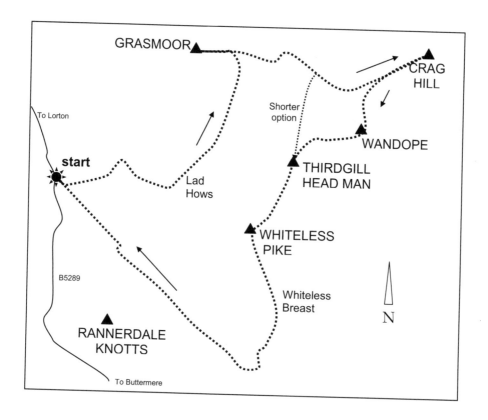

At Lad Hows the path turns left and, after a pleasant, almost level section, begins to climb more seriously again in heather. The route encounters some loose stone as it makes its way up the well-defined ridge but a little path which zig-zags across the stones makes progress much easier. The stony but pleasant onward way continues clearly and, except for a few upwards steps requiring care, without difficulty. Approaching the rocky summit of the ridge the way steepens and there is a choice of trodden paths or of climbing through short heather, stones and grass. The final section to the rocky tor is steepish, loose stone but the path again offers a helpful zig-zagging route. For just a few paces there is no escape from the worst of the scree, but taking it slowly and carefully choosing a way make it quite straightforward.

At the rocky tor the path arrives at the edge of Grasmoor's broad summit plateau and the nature of the climb changes completely. From here the way becomes gentle and grassy and the walking extremely simple. The summit is now quite close and the path swings slightly left to head towards it and reach a major path. Turn left onto it and in two minutes arrive at the top of Grasmoor, where there is a large shelter, but, surprisingly, no OS column.

The view is extensive in all directions, although the broadness of the summit plateau robs it of the drama of the vistas seen on the ascent. The cairn to the west of the summit and the smaller shelter to the south are worth visits for the views of Buttermere, Crummock and Loweswater, and an awful lot of hills.

Leave the top on the arrival path and continue on it as it runs round the edge of the plateau and over a cairned hump before dropping into a depression where there is a major crosspaths. For the shorter walk, turn right onto the clear path which climbs a little as it runs directly to the cairn on the summit of Thirdgill Head Man. But preferably go straight on and follow the path to the OS column on the summit of Crag Hill and then on south-eastwards a couple of cairns towards the ridge leading to Sail. From here is a magnificent view of Derwentwater, Blencathra and Skiddaw, the Causey Pike ridge, Barrow and Outerside, Grisedale Pike, the Langdales, Scafells and Gables.

Return to the column and again leave as you arrived, but where the path swings right to descend to the major crosspaths, go straight on and either descend on initially pathless grass to find a developing path a little lower down, or move left onto the thin path running close to the edge. Continue into the depression and bend left to continue round the rim of the crags (Addacomb Hole) and climb the short distance to the top of Wandope.

Leave on the path which heads off just south of west and walk to the cairn which is visible on the grassy hump of Thirdgill Head Man. Having paused here and looked over to our route of ascent with more than a little satisfaction, leave Thirdgill Head Man west of south on the only possible path and follow it down the ridge to the depression of Saddle Gate and on to the cairnless top of Whiteless Pike. From here there is a nice view of the Scafells, the Gables, and of the Buttermere hills round to Haystacks and Fleetwith Pike; the three lakes, Buttermere, Crummock Water and Loweswater are also all still in view.

Continue in the same direction on a clear path which drops, roughly at times, down towards Buttermere village. The roughness is best avoided

Grasmoor seen from Brackenthwaite Hows

by initially keeping to the right, and then, beyond an easier section of path with a very short stepped bit, moving left on a trod which loops round and descends easily to rejoin the main way. The gradient now becomes very gentle and a lengthy easy section follows. Rannerdale Knotts appears on the right, with the valley of Squat Beck, down which our way lies, in front of it. The path contours left round the hillside and begins to drop more steeply again. Then, as it descends into the dip at the end of the Rannerdale Knotts, it does a zig-zag left; here go straight on to join the main path which has come down from the col and begin the long gradual descent of the valley.

Ignore a stile on the right and continue on the main path to finally arrive at a gate in a wall on the left, where a National Trust sign tells that the "bluebells are an historic feature of Rannerdale". Go through the gate and, if you are fortunate enough to be here in May, into the carpet of blue flowers. The path crosses the footbridge, swings left and continues gently down the lower part of the valley to reach the ford where we started. Across the stream, one car park is on the left and the other just over the rise ahead.

Walk 33
The western fringe

Out on the western fringe of Lakeland, between the high mountains crowded around Pillar and the narrow coastal plain of the Irish sea, lies an area of rolling grassy upland which makes an ideal place for a peaceful walk on a bank holiday or summer weekend when the weather is clear but the well known hills are likely to be busy with tourists. It is a straightforward walk mostly on grass (plus a bit on forest tracks) which initially follows the high ground between the valleys of the Ehen and the Calder, to reach a high point which gives a glorious view of Ennerdale and its encircling mountains. Then, having also visited the highest hill hereabouts, the route returns on lower ground in the company of the infant River Calder.

Summits visited	Blakeley Raise (1276ft/389m) Grike (1601ft/488m) Crag Fell (1716ft/523m) Whoap (1676ft/511m) Lank Rigg (1775ft/541m)
Start	The Cold Fell Road, south of Ennerdale Bridge
Distance	7 miles/11.25km
Height gain	1850ft/560m
Time	5.5 hours
Map	OS Explorer OL4 (North-western)
Facilities	None

Parking: From a junction half a mile west of Ennerdale Bridge on the Cleator Moor road, a good minor road, signposted Gosforth and Calder Bridge, runs south across the shoulder of Cold Fell. After 2 miles/3km, at NY 067130, and at a useful elevation of 940ft/298m, the road does a right angle bend right and a rough track (signed Public Bridleway Kinniside Common) goes straight on. The walk starts from this corner. There is parking for a single vehicle in an unsurfaced lay-by just before the corner and for half a dozen more on the verge on the right just beyond the corner. The unfenced road presents various other parking opportunities further away from the corner, particularly on the Ennerdale Bridge side.

The walk
The walk starts with one of two short pathless sections. Having paused at the road corner to admire the view of the Isle of Man with Dent just to its right, strike off uphill (north-east) towards the highest point. Pass a ruined stone structure (marked 'bield' on the OS map) and continue to the top of Blakeley Raise, where there is a fence corner with a coniferous plantation beyond.

Leave the summit half-right on a clear trod with the fence on the left and follow it downhill. At the shallow depression skirt the wet area to follow the main path round a small fenced enclosure to a metal gate in the fence. Go through and along the track which runs besides trees to join a forest

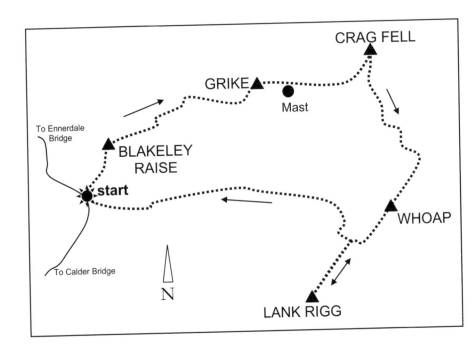

road. Turn right along it to walk with the forest on the right and a fence on the left. After around 0.5 mile/0.75km, a metal gate in the fence, which may have to be climbed, gives access to the slopes of Grike. Through, or over, the gate, an initially unclear thin path going half-right (east) rises up the grass slope to a rather awkward stile in a cross-fence. Cross this and advance a few paces to the top of Grike, where are found two large piles of stones, a substantial shelter, and, at last, a view of Lakeland. This is good, but nothing like as good as that from our next summit, Crag Fell.

So, leave Grike on the path which sets off eastwards. Ahead on the right can be seen a weather station with a short black mast, and beyond, the path running round the head of Ben Gill and across the shallow depression, keeping to the left of the accompanying fence. Beyond the depression, cross the (broken) stile in the cross-fence, and continue on the path which rises initially close to the fence and then swings left to the summit of Crag Fell. From here is the star view of the walk – Ennerdale Water enclosed by high hills, from Great Borne in the north-east, round to Steeple and Haycock in the south-east. This is a good place to sit and eat sandwiches.

Leave Crag Fell on the narrow path heading south. As you descend easily downhill towards a coniferous plantation, it is helpful to look ahead to the next section of the walk. The white OS column on our final summit, Lank Rigg, is clearly visible on the skyline, with our intermediate destination, Whoap, appearing as a hump in front of it. Looking beyond the trees ahead, a wall runs up the fellside and turns half-left to head off to the distant Caw Fell. Our route climbs from the trees on a path to the right of this wall, and follows it a little way past where it turns left before striking off right towards the top of Whoap.

Back in the present, the path now drops a little more steeply to a stile in a fence at the corner of a plantation. Go over the stile, perhaps with a little difficulty due to erosion on the downhill side, and continue on the clear path down through a clearing in the trees to reach a forest track at a marker cairn. Go left for just 25yds and then turn right on a thin track going down through a break in the trees and quickly becoming very clear. Emerging from the bottom of the plantation, the path swings left across some wet ground and then climbs as a stony track to a stile in a fence. Go over onto the open fellside and continue up the path to the right of the wall that was noted during the descent from Crag Fell. From the corner, striking up right would take you to the top of Whoap, but to avoid dips and hollows, and most of the wetness, prefer to continue by the wall for 100yds or so to the top of a rise just beyond a small gate in the wall. Here turn sharp right and head south-westwards through the long grass back towards the top of the ridge. Look on the left for the path coming down from Caw Fell and running along the ridge top; join it and follow it towards the high point ahead.

The path does not actually visit the top of Whoap but runs to its right towards a prominent white stone – which appears to be of no particular significance. A thin trod does fork off left to the highest point, but its start is extremely difficult to find. Therefore, step left off the main path as it approaches the top to find this thin trod and follow it over the highest point, the exact location of which is not marked and in doubt, and continue on it as it drops (west of south) down the grassy slope to the depression between Whoap and Lank Rigg. Ignore a path coming in from

The summit of Lank Rigg

the right, cross the col and continue up the grass slope opposite, to the summit of Lank Rigg, where there is an OS column and a pile of stones. The path continues in the same direction a short distance to a cairn on a rocky outcrop where a large tumulus, apparently of some historical interest, comes into view, and from which there is an excellent view down the coast to Black Coombe.

Retrace steps past the column and back down the grassy slope, enjoying the views across the Solway to Scotland, with Criffel now appearing directly over Grike. At the col turn left, and follow the narrow but very clear path as it drops gently into the valley, the long walk down which, on mostly grassy, but sometimes wet paths, is easy. Just before a ford across a significant side stream, our path joins a broad stony track coming down from the right. Now just a mile away from the car, our track reverts to grass as it continues gently on. Drop down to another ford and follow the track as it now parts company with the infant River Calder and begins its gradual climb out of the valley. At a fork, either way will do; they rejoin a little way further on. Soon the track levels and its end, at the road corner, comes into view just a minute away.

Walk 34
Ennerdale

Ennerdale is quite different from other major Lakeland valleys. Not only is it virtually untouched by tourism, but also its management is overseen and coordinated by a partnership of its primary land owners. The National Trust, Forestry Commission and United Utilities have formed the "Wild Ennerdale Partnership" with the vision "to allow the evolution of Ennerdale as a wild valley for the benefit of people relying more on natural processes to shape its landscape and ecology". More information is at **www.wildennerdale.co.uk**

This walk provides an introduction to the valley at both high and low levels. After a fairly strenuous climb, a simple walk along the broad grassy ridge between Ennerdale and Buttermere leads to a delightful streamside descent and an easy return along the valley floor beside the lake. There is a short easy scramble on the ascent, and the return to the valley starts with a pathless section, which would be tricky in poor visibility.

Summits visited	**Great Borne (2019ft/616m)** **Starling Dodd (2077ft/633m)** **Little Dodd (1936ft/590m)**
Start	**Bowness Knott, Ennerdale**
Distance	**7 miles/11.25km**
Height gain	**2070ft/630m**
Time	**5.5 hours**
Map	**OS Explorer OL4 (North-western)**
Facilities	**There are no facilities at Bowness Point except some picnic tables and the start of the 2 mile/3.3km Smithy Beck Trail; maps which promise toilets are long out-of-date. There is food and accommodation in Ennerdale Bridge, 4.25 miles/6.75km away**

Interestingly, neither ascent nor descent appears in the first edition of the Wainwright guides.

Parking: Park on the large free Forestry Commission car park at Bowness Knott (NY 109153). This is the furthest vehicles can be taken into the valley.

The walk

Return along the tarmac road for around 700yds to where, just beyond the large Forestry Commission sign, the road bends left. Here climb the stile on the right by a stream and join the clear grass path which climbs steeply past the corner of the forest fence to a fork. Take the left-hand branch and follow it up into the shallow dip between Great Borne and Brown How where, by a large angular boulder, there is another fork. Go left again, following the direction of Rake Beck, on a way which is now narrower but still clear.

After splitting into two and rejoining, the path arrives at an interesting and excellently preserved old structure, which is quite unlike any other in the District. It is generally described as an ancient fox trap, the fox being caught as it tried to retrieve a dead goose hung on a pole over the deep central chamber. There is a little knoll nearby which is worth a visit. Just by the trap, the path turns left and continues to climb, now a little

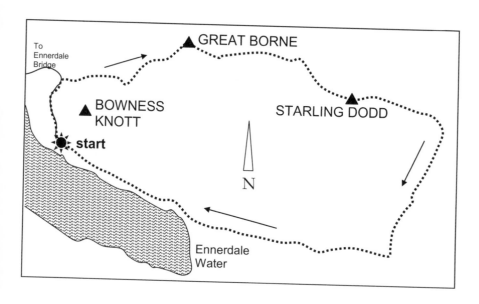

more eroded than it was lower down, towards a large crag. Near the top of the slope the way encounters a short, easy scramble, which can be traversed without difficulty by looking ahead and planning an easy way. The pleasant climb now stays close to the pretty stream as it falls down little cascades, and shortly arrives at the edge of the broad summit plateau. Here bend right with the path and follow it as it continues to rise gently to the stony summit of Great Borne, where there are a substantial shelter, an OS column built of red stone, and a fence. The good all-round view includes the Grasmoor group, the Gables and Pillar, the Solway with its mass of turbines, and the ridge continuing to High Stile along which lies our onward way.

Leave the summit with the column on the left and the shelter on the right and head towards the fence, swinging right before it is reached to follow a path which runs alongside it. In a few paces the fence and path are seen dropping down into the depression ahead where they both turn left; beyond, our way is clear to Starling Dodd – which is overtopped by Red Pike and High Stile. Beyond the corner, the path shortcuts an angle in the fence, and is then deflected to the right by it, around a small conservation area, to arrive at the foot of the final slope to Starling Dodd. The right-hand of the two continuing paths now leads quickly to the summit, where are found two cairns, one unusually being constructed from old metal fence posts as well as stone. Featuring in the view now are Scotland across the Solway, the Buttermere hills (with Grasmoor still prominent), the continuation of our ridge to Red Pike and High Stile, and the Ennerdale valley with the Gables at its head and its upper reaches dominated by Pillar.

Our next calling point is the minor hump of Little Dodd, which is the next high point along the ridge. So leave Starling Dodd maintaining the direction of arrival but moving left slightly to pick up the onward path. Continue into the depression, where there is a small triangular tarn, but here forsake the main path, which bends left round the flank of Little Dodd, and continue ahead to climb past a single fence post to its spiky cairn. Note the excellent views left to Crummock Water with the North-Western fells beyond.

To commence the descent back into the valley, continue in the same direction (eastwards) past the end of a line of old fence posts and press on over pathless terrain, bending right to descend the steepening slope into the little valley of Gillflinter Beck, aiming to meet up with the stream as soon as possible to avoid as much of the heather and stones as possible. Step across the stream and amble down slowly besides its many

The cairns on Starling Dodd

little cascades. The thoroughly delightful descent is initially pathless but, as the narrow valley begins to widen out, a trodden way develops which can be seen running ahead down into the valley through a broad break in the trees. Look for a large, sprawling pile of stones on the right-hand bank and here (or slightly higher) cross the stream easily. Pause to note the absolutely superb mountain architecture of the Gables, Kirk Fell and Pillar left across Ennerdale, and then continue down the clear grass path which moves right away from the stream and heads down the break in the forest to climb a stile in a cross-fence. Beyond, the path is lost in some wet ground but reappears running down the centre of the ride. Ignore stiles in the fences right and left. Pass a ruined fold and then hop across the little stream to a stile and gate which give access to the main valley track by a National Trust "Gillerthwaite" sign. Reassuringly, a Public Footpath waymark points back the way we have come.

Turn right onto the track for an easy and pleasant 2.5 miles/4km walk back to the car park at Bowness Knott, passing the Youth Hostel at High Gillerthwaite and then following the shore of Ennerdale Water.

Walk 35
The top of England

Do not miss out on visiting the highest land in the country simply because it is high. Certainly there is a lot of climbing and it is a popular destination, but this walk is neither long nor difficult. The route described avoids the crowds on the ascent by diverting over a neighbouring top which arguably gives the two most impressive and memorable mountain views in the District. The way has no difficulties other than steepness, and most of the climbing is on grass. The final section to Scafell Pike is unavoidably on loose stone but the gradients are not severe and although progress is slow and requires concentration, it is not difficult. The direct return is on a major route which has been extensively repaired and is easy throughout.

Summits visited	Lingmell (2649ft/807m) Scafell Pike (3210 ft/978m)
Start	Wasdale Head
Distance	5.5 miles/8.75km
Height gain	3250ft/990m
Time	6.25 hours
Map	OS Explorer OL6 (South-western)
Facilities	The Wasdale Head Inn is 1 mile/1.5km away at the head of the valley

Parking: Park in the National Trust's pay and display car park (NY 182075) adjacent to their campsite at Wasdale Head. The entrance to both campsite and car park is on the right travelling towards Wasdale Head, not far beyond the head of the lake and opposite a small parking area on the left (which fills up first as it avoids paying the charge). There is a sign at the road end "Wasdale Head Hall Farm", and a finger post "Public Footpath Scafell Massif, Eskdale". Having turned off the main road, approach is by a single track unsurfaced lane which crosses Lingmell Beck on a bridge with a decidedly temporary look.

The walk

Continue up the track, cross a cattle grid and go through a gate marked "Wasdale Head Hall Farm". Cross a wide wooden bridge over Lingmell Gill and keep left (signed Eskdale, Miterdale, Scafell Massif) and walk up the track with the gill on your left. At the fork go left again (signed Permitted Path Scafell) and pass to the left of Brackenclose (a climbing hut). Continue uphill to a wooden footbridge; cross it and go through the gate. The path swings right and continues uphill towards a kissing gate. Here pause to survey the way ahead. Immediately beyond the kissing gate our route bears left off the main path and climbs the long steep grassy ridge, going over a ladder stile half way up, continuing right along the plateau to Lingmell, and across the col to Scafell Pike, the western wall of which faces us. The jagged lump further to the right is Scafell, and is not on our itinerary for today.

Wasdale Head and Mosedale from the ladder stile on the climb to Lingmell

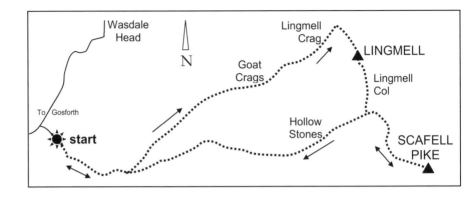

So, go up to and through the kissing gate and immediately leave the main path to follow the grassy path rising left and making its way up the ridge. Cross a clear path contouring round the hillside and continue steeply up to the ladder stile. Over this a short detour of a few paces left gives a nice view over Wasdale Head with its interesting field system, and with the wall and fence as foreground makes quite a good photograph.

A little further up, the path traverses a short stony section which in places is quite loose, so some minor diversions may be helpful. Then, somewhat perversely, as the path becomes grassy again, there are some rather nice stone steps. Soon the gradient eases and the walking becomes very straightforward on an easy grass plateau. Goat Crags come into view ahead.

At a fork keep left (although note that the narrower right-hand way makes a useful short cut across to the return path if the weather is deteriorating) to approach and then easily climb the low crags above, aided on the sometimes faint way by a series of cairns. A broken wall comes into view, and beyond it a rocky, spiky skyline, which is the summit ridge of Lingmell. Over on the right is the major path which we forsook at the intake wall, coming up into the col between Lingmell and Scafell Pike and swinging up right to climb to the top of the latter. We shall use this path, after visiting the summit of Lingmell, to climb to the top of Scafell Pike, and, later, for our return to the valley.

Advance to, and cross the broken wall on a clear way. The summit of Lingmell now lies ahead at the right hand end of the summit ridge and could be approached directly. However, infinitely to be preferred is to first visit the elegant, magnificently-sited cairn which can be seen half-left on the skyline, and then to walk right along the ridge to the summit. To do this use the path which heads off from the broken wall in the desired direction through a patch of coarse grass. This soon peters out, but beyond it can be seen a grassy shelf running across the hillside which will provide a way to the cairn without needing to negotiate too many boulders. So continue, initially making a bee-line for the cairn, and then when it disappears from view, heading for the grassy shelf. Once on the shelf, look right for an easy way to climb the short distance up the summit ridge to the cairn on its left-hand end.

The cairn is found to be an absolutely splendid, beautifully built structure positioned near the edge of a significant precipice from where one looks across to the magnificent southern face of Great Gable rising over 2000ft/610m from Lingmell Beck.

From here, walk east of south along the summit ridge (heading towards the summit of Scafell Pike beyond). There are various bits of trods and sheep-tracks to help on the way but surprisingly no definitive path initially. The first rocky lump which appears to be the summit isn't, so, as it looks a little awkward to climb, go round to its right where you will see a second, much more accessible lump with the significant summit cairn on top. Approaching the summit rocks there is, down on the left, a stupendous view down a gulley in Lingmell Crag and into the depths of Piers Gill below. Or keep right, away from the edge, to avoid this slightly exposed section of path and its attendant excitement.

After the dramatic views of Great Gable and Piers Gill which have been experienced from nearby, the panorama from the summit may seem a bit ordinary. However, the fells around Wasdale Head are good, as are Scafell and Scafell Pike, the summit of the latter looking reassuringly close. And beneath our feet, the considerable drop down to Piers Gill cannot fail to impress.

Leave the top southwards and find a clear path heading down into the col. Although initially grassy, this quickly becomes an unpleasant ribbon of stones. So forsake the path for the adjacent grass and at the bottom of the main slope go ahead across the hollow on a faint path in grass. Cross the broken wall at the obvious crossing point, and follow the thin path up the grass slope to the right of some big rocks, to join the stony, and normally busy, major path, just where it swings uphill, to the top of Scafell Pike.

This being the highest point in the country, the view is, unsurprisingly extensive, but, apart from the novelty of being able to see so many hills and valleys, it is not particularly attractive; neither is the necessity of sharing it with a seething mass of humanity and the majority of their dogs. But do linger; it is a special place. And do note that you are a long way short of the ages of at least some of the people here, and quietly rejoice in the prospect of many more years of visiting high places!

Leave the top north-westwards, on the path on which you arrived and retrace your steps to the col. On the way there is a fork where you need to keep right. The descent over stones is not difficult if you adopt an easy pace. Approaching the col, swing left with the main path which will now take you all the way back to the car. Here, with the worst of the crowds left behind, the gradient eases and the walking becomes much easier. Very soon the path becomes wide with a smooth compacted surface, and then stepped, paved or pitched virtually all the way down.

Arriving at the intake wall, go through the kissing gate and keep left to continue down beside the stream. Having sampled many varieties of pitching and paving on the descent, on this flatter section the path appears untidy and neglected although the surroundings on the streamside are quite pretty. Arrive at a kissing gate with an interesting padlocked box, and note that this is where we branched up the grass to the ridge top on our outward journey. So go through the kissing gate and keep close to the fence side and slightly left of the broad track to shortly arrive at, and cross over, the footbridge. Once over the bridge and descending with the stream on your right, the return to the car is straightforward.